Praise for THE DISAPPEARANCE

"*The Disappearance* may read like a tragic comedy, but at its heart it is a timely tale about desperation, revolutionary dreams, and a journey to triumph over the darkness that lies within us all."

—**Jonathan Evison,** *New York Times* bestselling author

"An intriguing account of a man who disappeared, then reappeared...beautifully written, deeply self-reflective, tantalizing, and layered with levels of mystery. Things are not always as they appear, as Steven Kubacki wrestles with what happens to him (and with his own actions) and strives to make sense of it all."

—**Alan Tjeltveit,** psychology professor emeritus at Muhlenberg College

"*The Disappearance* is Charles Dickens's *A Christmas Carol* on acid with hints of Carlos Castaneda, Jack Kerouac, and the wandering, road-hungry Woody Guthrie. Our protagonist, Steve Kubacki (Ebenezer Scrooge), is redeemed just as he was becoming Nathan (Jacob Marley). In terms the Beat poets and Timothy Leary fans would understand (but Dickens might wonder at), Kubacki was restored and lifted to a higher plane of human existence by finding the holy grail: interdependence in others. The resulting outflowing of compassion, the loss of the exaggerated self, the palpable celebration and triumph of agape love, make the conclusion inspiring."

—**Linden DeBie,** PhD, author of *Dorian, Rip's Knickerbockers, Speculative Theology and Common-Sense Religion*, and several edited works on American religion and philosophy

"Steve Kubacki wrote the most intriguing book... I really immersed myself in this book and this must-read story that leads to questioning how much of reality we really understand, and what choices we have in shifting out of the states of illusion we are in now to living a life filled with light."

—**Sandra Ingerman,** MA, international shamanic teacher and author of thirteen books, including *Soul Retrieval*

THE DISAPPEARANCE

OTHER BOOKS BY STEVEN KUBACKI

Steven Kubacki and Brian Blackmore, *Meta-Mathematical Foundations of Existence: Gödel, Quantum, God & Beyond* (Kindle, 2017)

THE DISAPPEARANCE

Conspiracy, Revolution, Revelation…

The Extraordinary Disappearance
of Steven Kubacki
(After 45 Years of Silence)

BY STEVEN KUBACKI, PHD

with Dylan James Quarles

Miami

Published by Mango Publishing, a division of Mango Publishing Group, Inc.

Cover Design: Roberto Nunez
Cover Photos: Thomas Renner, Steven Kubacki
Layout & Design: Megan Werner

For permission requests, please contact the publisher at:
Mango Publishing Group
5966 South Dixie Highway, Suite 300
Miami, FL 33143
info@mango.bz

For special orders, quantity sales, course adoptions and corporate sales, please email the publisher at sales@mango.bz. For trade and wholesale sales, please contact Ingram Publisher Services at customer.service@ingramcontent.com or +1.800.509.4887.

The Disappearance: Conspiracy, Revolution, Revelation… The Extraordinary Disappearance of Steven Kubacki (After 45 Years of Silence)

Library of Congress Cataloging-in-Publication number: 2025938460
ISBN: (hc) 978-1-68481-856-3 (e) 978-1-68481-857-0
BISAC category code: TRU006000 TRUE CRIME / Abductions, Kidnappings & Missing Persons

Printed in the United States of America

This book is dedicated to all people who are trying to make the world a better place creatively, entrepreneurially, politically, and economically and to those who study, explore, and experience the multiverse, within which our universe is but one of many.

Steven Kubacki vanished without a trace in 1978, only to walk out of a field fifteen months later, claiming no recollection of anything that happened to him. In the decades since, millions of people have speculated about what happened, but Kubacki has never spoken about that "lost" time...until now.

The Disappearance is the dramatic and never-before-revealed true account of how an idealistic college student went out onto the ice of Lake Michigan and never really came back.

TABLE OF CONTENTS

Prologue

SKIING ONTO THE ICE

The lengthened evenings
ring the memories
of future dreams, a dream in rain and ice embraced.
The initiation of trying to be:
Scientist, lover, friend,
conversationalist, mystic, explorer.
Sick of this no-will-be succession
of perverse I-ams.
Betraying an ad-hoc insistence
Betraying a sing-to-me-lullaby identity.
And I am thinking
my tent erected in the Lindenhof
a colorless sunset
in a place I-believe-I-think-I-know
I'm here

—Steven Kubacki, 1976

February 19, 1978

I've set my skis to the west, weaving through rattling pines where ice-laden branches can be heard quivering in the bitter wind. Undeterred, my tracks break past this last defense of life and cross the snow-covered sand to the ice. Ice floes have drifted onto the beach for weeks, crashing, piling themselves high in December and January. Now, in February, they have fused into an expansive wasteland that extends miles into Lake Michigan.

This is dead winter, and I can't see another living being. Later in the day, a few students like me might cross-country ski through the fields, over fences and dunes, to the edge of the frozen lake. I did this as often as I could, compelled by a desire to transcend the academic borders of bland discovery. The bleak and loveless snow offered a scholastic antithesis.

I almost never met people on the lake at this time of morning, however, and that was good. Those drawn to these early hours had either departed south to vegetate in the sun, or they were here hibernating in the fortresses of fear and love we call homes. Only fools ventured across the frozen plains now, because the chance of vanishing until spring was a risk few would dare.

At twenty-three, my concept of mortality is abnormally heightened. I have faced death many times before. Each one prepared me for this moment.

Patterned by serpentine gusts of wind, the snowy expanse stretches on until it meets the distant horizon. In between, the ice rises, shaped by the waves of the lake. That same force, as powerful as gravity, wind, and earth, pushes me forward now.

Just past the line where the water, had it still been water, would meet the shore, a ridge rises in the outline of a bell, five meters above the lake's surface. Beyond, a half mile distant, is another ridge, twice as high, a towering juxtaposition of angular blocks and jutting triangles—massive and treacherous. The protrusions cast by shifting ice and drifting snow are sculpted like sandstone carvings in the wind.

Overhead, the pale February sun does little to dull the cutting cold, yet at first, I hardly notice it. My mind and my heart are focused on what lies ahead. My arms extend and push off the poles, my knees bent and my torso crunched, my weight shifting from one leg to the next. A familiar rhythm develops.

The frozen ground whispers warnings as I slide onto it, the shifting of unseen forces. Now, moving into my rhythm, I gain speed, one ski chasing the other. The pitted surface of the frozen lake evokes a sense of lunar desolation.

I picture myself as a lone astronaut, beyond the brink of civilization, abandoned, skiing into the shadow of a serrated ice shelf. The morning has grown colder, and the wind cuts cruelly through my clothes, numbing my skin. A part of me enjoys this elemental coldness. Another aspect of me pushes me to keep going, relentless and unwavering.

I have an eerie feeling of being watched—that someone or something has eyes on me. No matter how far I get from the lonely shoreline and the sleepy college town I deplore, I feel this presence.

Perhaps it is the spirit of the place itself, which some call the Michigan Triangle. This corner of the country has a reputation. Locals have claimed to see strange lights in the sky at night, and there were whispers about animals walking upright through dense shoreline forests. Venture too far on the concentric rings of winter ice, some said, and who knows what you might encounter. The schooner *Thomas Hume* and its crew of seven vanished here in 1891, and thirty years later, the two-masted *Rosabelle* would be found floating, bottom up, in calm waters. There was no storm reported or sign of a collision, but the eleven men who had set sail were missing and never found. Then Captain George Donner of the *O.S. McFarland* freighter retired to his stateroom one night in 1937 and disappeared. His crew swore under oath that the door was locked from the inside and the porthole was far too small for a man to squeeze through. When Northwest Airlines Flight 2501 vanished over the Michigan Triangle on June 23, 1950, police reported a red orb hovering above the lake.

I didn't know any of those stories at the time. And it was still years before professor of underwater archaeology Mark Holley discovered in 2007 what looked like a sunken Stonehenge resting on the lakebed, with monoliths that resembled mastodons.

What I did not know does not matter.

The inevitable drives me forward, until I find the place.

Alone on the frozen tundra, I hear a strange sound. It begins like a low-pitched whine carried by the wind, then morphs into a throbbing uproar. I look at the next rampart of ice, wondering if some kind of engine is coming toward me, before realizing that the uncanny sound is coming from my own head—a resonance within—that seems to spread itself like sound waves over the ice.

The sun melts and glazes the surface of the lake, so it looks like shattered pieces of glass that shimmer together, with every jagged detail unique but connected. On the reflections of this endless mirror, diabolical fantasies are released, daring me to join. In the expanding nowhereness, a faint glow begins to fill my peripheral vision.

My mind, steeped in the philosophy of the infinite and mired in the emotional pressure of the past few weeks, is more than primed to perceive the extraordinary. The ice comes to life. I become immobile as great shelves of ice surround and engulf me. In awe, I watch an occurrence I can only call "auroral intensity" unfolding before my eyes.

Over time, my memory of what happened next has undergone several revisions, updated by fragments freed from depths of unintended repression. I remember a seam in the air, a separating of sky from sky, like the parting of thick curtains. I recall a large object above me—or was it just the feeling of an object?

Does the interpretation matter?

Time ceases to exist, and materialization—the physicality the mind demands—does not follow for a while. Rooted to the spot, I am overcome by a kaleidoscope of conflicting possibilities, of hopes and fears I forget one after another. My eyes begin to water uncontrollably, and in the frigid air, I see the hands on my wristwatch. Are they moving?

The ice then cracks, gunshot loud in the still air! A wave of frigid cold envelops me, and I encounter a vague feeling of drifting that seems like forever—or was it only a second?

Imperceptibly, the drifting stops. I remember something like a caressing and rhythmic pressure comforting my body. I sense an avalanche of snowy images—icy thoughts descending like millions of snowflakes. They crash and thunder down the slopes of something shiny like metal into my brain, lights turning off and on at different angles. They seem to be everywhere but hidden, secret, burying me beneath their illuminations, in a complexity I cannot disentangle, cannot even locate—am I under the water, on the ice, in the sky, where? In space? I need an answer.

"Not yet," I hear someone say but cannot locate. As if I asked but did not.

Chapter 1
THE DISAPPEARANCE

They dug a trench but found no bodies
Instead, their shovels lifted huge piles
of dust
Enough to build a bridge
of certainty

Onto it they scampered
the lemmings
of imagination

remembering
too
late
that
they
were
once
human

—From the Nexalistic Revolutionary Front (NRF)
Documents by Nathan T. Stanfield (NTS)
a.k.a. Steven Kubacki, 1978

On Monday, February 20, 1978, at about eleven in the morning, a group of snowmobilers came across my skis, poles, and backpack near the town of Saugatuck, in a remote area of the Lake Michigan shoreline. They reported that footprints, barely visible beneath the fresh-fallen snowfall, tracked off for 200 yards before coming to an abrupt and unsettling end near the place where the frozen waves rose as high as thirty or forty feet. Deep crevices formed between those mounds, and the ice was thin.

One snowmobiler rushed to a nearby construction site, where workers were endeavoring to turn the once stately St. Augustine Seminary into a medium security prison. He called the police.

Trooper Honcharenko of the Michigan State Police, South Haven station, arrived within an hour, and the snowmobilers showed him what they'd discovered. They had not opened my pack, still slightly snow-covered, or moved anything. They'd looked around the area, venturing as far onto the ice as the first frozen wave, but had not seen any sign of a person, which concerned them. The ice beyond was too thin to safely support human weight, they warned the officer.

Horachenko described the scene as orderly. "The skis were side by side, facing the lake, about eight inches apart. The ski poles were stuck in the snow upright on the outside of the skis. The blue backpack was sitting on top of the skis. The backpack was fully packed." One ski, the officer noted, had a Deerfield, Massachusetts address printed on it.

The backpack revealed more clues: "a pair/black, thickly insulated gloves; brown bag containing lunch; a rolled-up plastic bag (one big one small); a plastic canteen; a cigar box containing miscellaneous items; a notebook pad with loose sheets of writing paper (some written) and college handout material; also, a drawing pad."

The officer zeroed in on a dentist's bill for a cavity filling. It was dated February 3, 1978, and addressed to Mr. Steven Kubacki.

South Haven desk officers followed up with the dentist, Robert C. Ackerman, who informed them that I was a student at Hope College in the nearby town of Holland. He also provided my phone number, but when the police called, there was no answer.

At 2:30 p.m., Holland Police knocked on the door of my attic apartment at 646 Church Street, but no one was home. They contacted Hope College authorities, who checked with my professors and reported that I had not attended any classes that day.

The police then sought out my roommate, James Courtier, who told them he hadn't seen me since midday Saturday, when I'd mentioned that I was going cross-country skiing. No, he did not think I was despondent or worried about anything specific. When I didn't return, James said he assumed I was on another of my overnight expeditions, given my proclivity for thrill-seeking and outdoor adventuring. He reported I typically carried a pup tent in my backpack, and that he'd been with me on previous trips when I'd gone as far as two miles out onto the ice, alone, while he waited on shore.

It was only when the police began talking about search planes and helicopters that James seemed to register that something serious had happened. His face drained of color, and he started to sweat despite the cold.

The State Police called in Search and Rescue and the Coast Guard, yet with only two hours of daylight remaining, there was little hope that air support would make it to the remote part of the lake before nightfall. To aid the rescue, Hope College chartered a local private plane, a Cessna 172, to make sweeps of the area. For over an hour in the growing darkness, it wheeled back and forth in the sky above the tangled forests that rimmed the lake, attempting to penetrate the snarl with its glaring spotlight. According to the official report, it had "nil results."

Later that night, the Dean of Students, Mike Gerrie, phoned my parents, who were divorced but still lived near each other in Massachusetts, to tell them that I was missing. John Kubacki and Irene Pegg (my mother had recently remarried) immediately rushed to the airport and got on a red-eye flight, arriving in Holland on Tuesday morning.

By that point, the lakefront was a frenzy of activity. As soon as the morning fog lifted, the Coast Guard and State Police both sent helicopters to buzz miles of frozen wilderness. Volunteer search parties, including many of my friends and classmates, combed the shoreline, where snow drifted up to four feet deep among the trees. My father was always among them, except when he was in the helicopters above, scanning the snow-covered ground. My close friend Richard Turner flew in from Georgia, and my childhood friend Charles Zane made the twelve-hour drive from Massachusetts.

According to the official report, all of Tuesday's detailed search efforts led to "nil results."

A Hope police officer interviewed James Courtier again. According to the officer's notes, James said that "he is sure that Kubacki went through the ice," but also "states that he was rather odd and it would not surprise him if he would take off to parts unknown." That couldn't be the case this time, though, James said, because he was sure I would never leave without telling him. We were best friends and told each other everything. As proof, James described the time I'd taken off the semester before to travel to Europe for two weeks. Although it was a fairly impulsive adventure, he reported that I had consulted with him about my itinerary, and he had given me money for the trip.

Another friend, Shelly McFerson, reported that she'd seen me on Friday evening at her house. She remembered me as being "in good spirits" and talking about plans for the coming week. Her story seemed compelling to the investigators, who noted in the report that they believed I'd "fallen through the ice and ha[d] not intentionally disappeared as some are inclined to believe."

For two days, seasoned trackers combed every inch of frozen shoreline, every shaded gully, and every pitted hollow. Divers suspended from ropes descended into the fissures in the ice, risking life and limb to probe its murky depths and look for suspicious places where the surface had broken. Teams of dogs hunted for a scent. No one found anything save for that single set of footprints dead-ending in the middle of the lake, which the professionals deemed too treacherous to search on foot.

Things started to look dire. The searchers began to whisper the story of a Hope College professor; a few years before, he had gone fishing at the lakeshore. He never came back. The official report was that he waded into the water and was dragged out by the tide. His body washed back to shore months later in the spring melt.

The South Haven police contacted the local authorities in my hometown of South Deerfield, Massachusetts, to find out if I had any fingerprints on file. (I did not.) They asked the helpful dentist if he had X-rays of my teeth. (He did.) The mood had shifted from "rescue" to "recovery."

On Wednesday afternoon, with the weather souring and hope of a happy ending becoming more and more unlikely, the authorities officially called off the search, though the State Police promised to have their pilots keep an eye out whenever they were in the area. Their decision understandably upset my parents, who tried to convince the volunteers to keep searching, but an air of acceptance had begun to taint the scene. The general assumption was that I had fallen into one of the frozen lake's deep crevices and drowned. If so, like the professor, my body was not likely to be found until spring or summer, after the thaw.

Every hour, fewer people took to the ice. Finally, Dean Gerrie convinced my parents that it was time to go home. No more could be done.

"I think they have to come to the realization that their son is gone," he told reporters. "But I'm sure they will continue to hope until the body is found."

Still, my father told a local newspaper, "As far as I'm concerned, Stevie's not dead until he's proven dead... He could have been dazed or hurt and wandered away from his equipment."

My friend Richard lingered after my parents left. A few months later, the school sent my parents a diploma, honoring me with the degree I was just three months from completing.

For the next few months, helicopters occasionally circled the area of the lake where I disappeared, waiting for my body to wash up. It never did.

By November, when no further discoveries were made, the missing persons case regarding my whereabouts was marked "inactive," much to my family's dismay. The local police had other more pressing matters.

They did make one last effort, though. In February 1979, the Michigan State Police contacted the sheriff's office in Chicago, shortly after the remains of dozens of victims of serial killer John Wayne Gacy were found in the crawl space of his home. "Please advise what address we can send dental records for possible ID for the remaining bodies not yet identified. Or pls advise what department is conducting the investigation if not yours. We have a Missing Person Complaint from 2/20/78. It is our understanding that Gacy was in our area about time of report." As far as I can tell, they received no response.

***

About a couple of years before my disappearance, I wrote this:

I, Steven Robert Kubacki, being sane and healthy, write my last will and testament.

To James Courtier, I bequeath all my books, writings, and documents, wherever they may be. I ask all my relatives and friends to assist James Courtier in retrieving all my books, documents, and writings promptly. I also bequeath to James Courtier all rights to publishing and copy write [sic] of my writings and papers. I grant these rights to no one else except James Courtier. James Courtier will however make accessible all my books, writings, and papers to all members of my immediate family: father, mother, brother, and sister, and to Jami Bozek. These letters, books, and writings shall not leave the premises where James Courtier has decided to place them.

To Jami Bozek, my dear cousin, I bequeath my camping equipment.

To my Father, John J. Kubacki, Senior, I bequeath all my money, income tax refunds, any proceeds from insurance. To my mother, Mrs. Irene Pegg, I leave all my love.

I also bequeath all my paintings, drawings, and art objects to James Courtier, to dispose of which as he pleases. Furthermore, I designate James Courtier as my spiritual heir.

These bequeathals are irrevocable and unalterable. They who dare to challenge the veritability and sincerity of this will are cursed.

If, however, James Courtier is dead, legally dead, or not to be found, all bequeathals in this will which he would have inherited are transferred to Jami Bozek, in trust for a period of three years, after which if James Courtier has not yet claimed his bequeathals, Jami Bozek will own and control.

Signed: Steven Kubacki
December 14, 1977

* * *

A few months before my disappearance, I elaborated:

Last Testament: I, the brother of brothers, sister of sisters, the Big Toe, the Thumb, hereby bequeath to the powerful — predatory impotency over others; on the altar of obedience I gift rebellion; to the delusional upbeat — the darkness that cripples; to slave drivers of expediency — a broken stopwatch; to the morality of indifference — the emptiness inside us; to corporate cathedrals — economic poverty; to well behaved academics — pretentious knowing. My soul, I donate to the NRF; my body parts to Walter — talismans in sacrifice to the good. My throne I abdicate to cliché minds and relinquish the Crown of Ignorance and Objectivity to know-it-alls. Let my body be trampled on, homage to necessary change. But let no whisper of my name be known, for I have none. For I am somewhere else, that no one knows.

Feeling like a tool, a tool I can't comprehend, a tool of interdimensional forces.

—From the Nexalistic Revolutionary Front (NRF)
Documents by Nathan T. Stanfield (NTS)
a.k.a. Steven Kubacki, 1978

Chapter 2
THE REEMERGENCE

We must be prepared

never

to return

to forget

who we are

in

a cloud of forgetting

in

a cloud of the unknown

—From the Nexalistic Revolutionary Front (NRF)
Documents by Nathan T. Stanfield (NTS)
a.k.a. Steven Kubacki, 1978

Fifteen months after my disappearance, on May 5, 1979, I find myself lying in a field of grass, my eyes closed, feeling the bitter gusts of the Lake Michigan wind, even as the summer sun warmed my face. I am filled with fragments from many different timelines, maybe dreams, intruding on the present.

I have forgotten a lot of the details from that day, assuming the specifics were ever my memories at all. How did I get there? What did I say? Fleeting associations and images danced before me—some like windows to other images, to other windows—personal narratives to structure and ground the self and capture the real, to make sure it was real.

A voice in my head eventually tells me to open my eyes, that it is time. When I do, I find myself surrounded by wildflowers in full bloom.

I shake my head to silence the voice. It is no longer the time for those images. I look at the backpack by my feet, pull out the books, journals, and maps. Thumbing through them, strange passages in my own handwriting leap out to me, bits of manifesto and madness.

"When will the ice that interlocks reason melt, and their fluids gasify into random molecules of incoherency and aimlessness, drifting and waiting for the coming assemblage of their purposes and with that concerted action?"

Then later:

"I am a patient revolutionary. We have only just begun to take chances."

There are other writings, descriptions of places and people—temples atop floating mountains and snake worshippers with the power to drain a person's bodily energy. It is a lot to take in, too outlandish and dangerous for anyone, even me, to read just yet. I bury the journals and promise to come back for them later. I keep the maps.

I look down at what I am wearing and feel a pang of distress. My clothes are filthy and tattered, and I probably need a shave. This is not the way I want to look, not for what I must do.

I have no plan. Why am I in this field? Why here? Did I fall asleep?

But there is no time left.

I flag down a passing car, ask for a ride. Hitchhiking was still a thing people did easily back then. The motions feel natural to me. Was hitchhiking how I got myself to the field? I don't remember clearly. I still don't.

The driver, a talkative and nosy fellow, says his name was Ronald. "What's yours?"

What do I tell him? Later, he would tell reporters that I introduced myself as Nathan, but that didn't make sense. I am Steven.

Ronald continues to ask questions. Where am I heading? Where have I been? I am wary, unprepared. *Where have I been? That might take a lifetime to reassemble.* I counter with questions of my own. *Where are we?* But I should know that. I must know that. *What is the town, the state?* I see a newspaper. *Is this today's date, today's year?*

Ronald tells me that we are on the road to Great Barrington, Massachusetts, and that the year is 1979. The newspaper I have agrees. Current facts and past impossible facts seem to cozy up to each other, trying to confuse me. Fifteen months?

Maybe there is something peculiar in the air—a simple explanation I could snuggle up to. But I know that the days of simple explanations are long past for me. What has happened, what is happening, is something beyond the realm of simple explanation.

I struggle to stay calm, while inside an ocean of disjointed memories compete for my attention. I think about the lake, frozen and empty, and at the same time flowing and full of life and vitality. I close my eyes.

The motorist later said that I told him I'd flown from San Francisco to Boston and then took a bus. When he mentioned that he was a seminary student, I told him about being in a cult. I supposedly told him I was going to talk to "a friend" with news about "a mutual missing acquaintance." I have no recollection of saying any of those things. But as I said, my mind was dissociated, uncertain. My past was locked in a container of intersecting times that were neither in the past, present, or future.

In the space of time that feels like a blink, I open my eyes again and discover that the nosy driver is gone, having left me at a roadside gas station. Thankfully, he didn't try to help me by taking me to a shelter or calling 911.

I consider the phone booth that stands in the parking lot for a space of time that feels eternal, although it is unoccupied save for the countless voices that reside within its wires and tubes. Something about its glass walls, enclosed and coffin-like, stirs visions of being sealed inside a sterile chamber—deep underground, or in the sky? There is a witch, or something like one. She takes my power, cleanses it of impurities, and gives it back.

The dark presence does not neglect me. Waves of forgetfulness roar in my ears. I tremble. Thank you. The box in front of me becomes simply a pay phone again.

In that moment, I affix my mind to the Velcro ground that lies beneath my feet, attaching me to the kindness of linear time. Time plods ever forward, even if my reality spins on an axle of chaos.

I walk inside the gas station and borrow the change to make my call. It clinks metallically as it feeds into the machine, the dial tone followed by the series of rotary clicks. I spin the long-remembered numbers before I lose my nerve.

Are they listening? Do they already know of my return?

I do not call my mother or my father first, though I am just seventy miles from them. That would be too great of a shock, both for them and for me. Instead, I call my Aunt June, calculating that she is one step removed from the emotional onslaught that will ensue.

* * *

It's only been recently, with forty-five years of distance and hindsight, that I have been able to go back and read the media reports that circled and surrounded my disappearance and reemergence. At the time, I avoided all of the coverage. I couldn't look at a newspaper for weeks without being blindsided by my own name. I felt deeply embarrassed and wished none of it was public. Now, I'm surprised to discover how much the journalists got wrong, especially about May 5. I've seen articles that say Ronald dropped me off directly at my father's house, and others where I never hitchhiked or met him at all but instead walked right from the field to Aunt June's house. The details conflict; they cannot all be true. I suspect reporters, racing to meet deadlines, confabulated the details they gathered or hastily arrived at them to produce a seamless story.

Comparatively, my own memories emerge in a discontinuous manner, separated and compartmentalized from each other, as if the images they present were a bunch of marbles laid out in a straight line. Between each marble or memory are my periods of dissociation, events not easily accessible, which, as a psychologist, I've learned is standard for times of intense and overwhelming experience. But here is what I remember happening:

Aunt June picks up the phone on the seventh ring. Half an hour later, her station wagon screeches into the gas station, sending up a turbulent cloud of noxious dust. She is sobbing, and her embrace is equal parts disbelieving and joyful.

I don't know what to say, so I say nothing. I cannot overcome the powerful swells of anticipation that freeze me in anxiety about the events to unfold—a tsunami I have unleashed yet now have little control over. What will I say? What *could* I say?

Aunt June talks nonstop as she frantically drives, filling me in on fifteen months of this and that, compressed into one hour. Like water through a sieve, it all passes through me. Eventually, she turns her station wagon down a shaded drive in South Deerfield. My father's house—the house I had grown up in—materializes halfway down Mountain Road, somehow different from the other houses. Haloed by the glow of nostalgia, it evokes memories of the time before—of another life, one without cataclysmic change—a life with the usual happinesses, sadnesses, failures, and triumphs.

I try to center myself, to sort through memories for answers to inevitable questions, answers not as reliable as this situation will surely demand. I am so flawlessly detached. Wake up, Steve, you've had the entire car ride—or the past fifteen months—to prepare for this! Yet all I know about what to say is what I've already told myself—that I woke up in a field with no recollection of what happened since the lake. It is all that I can and want to remember.

"I was somewhere cold and dark" is all I can come up with. Even that hangs heavy in my throat. I don't know how I will say that again and again, and I knew that I had to. No matter how unsatisfying, it would be immensely more palatable than the fragmented memories stalking my mind.

My head throbs, threatening to split my brain open like a puzzle box whose cypher is not complex enough to protect its contents from the tinkering of others. Would food or water help? I don't know.

"I phoned your dad before I left. Your mom is on the way, too." Aunt June's words focus me like a punch to the face. My anxiety multiplies. My mother would hear my words and see them for what they were, simple knots she could easily pick apart. Not a single sentence will stand her test. This fear pulls me out of stasis and into action. I think clearly. Weave a story into a net of simplicities, through which the complex truth cannot be found or slip out unexpectedly. I learned that trick from political orators I read in college, both revolutionaries and stalwarts of the status quo.

With a jolt, we pull up to the house, the front door flies open, and a man stumbles out. My father—generally animated, kind of manic—is crying, weeping with joy. Framed in the darkness he leaves behind him, I sense shapeless forms, rainbows of shadow, incomprehensible swirls that only I can sense, though they are many yards away from me. They gently tug at me, trying to draw me into dimensions of space beyond the four of everyday space—height, width, depth, and linear time. I resist. Many times in the past year these rainbows have visited me, sometimes in color. I have many hypotheses. Within their energetic clusters, they transfer information on waves of light into a biochemical form resembling that of human memories. Know-it-all psychologists would of course have other hypotheses.

However, this is not the place to dwell in the non-ordinary. Navigators of interdimensional time shells do not exist for Aunt June or my father. I discipline my mind and concentrate. Stay in the everyday world of family, their timeline in the multiverse.

Like watching a film projected on the opaque veil of my detachment, I watch us all walk up the stairs into my father's house. It feels strange receiving so much love from this man, so much uncharacteristic tenderness. I want to appreciate his tears, return his love, but my heart feels like a log just split by an ax waiting for someone to gather the pieces to burn.

Aunt June leaves the two of us standing in the living room and moves off into the kitchen to phone the rest of the family. From the corner, a flash bulb pops, and I realize that we aren't alone. A man with a camera—a reporter? He is in the room with us, capturing the reunion. Or is he? Perhaps he came later, the next day.

The room turns incandescent, and suddenly I am sitting on the couch, my father kneeling before me. He asks question after question. I can see him seeking answers, but also aware of others taking notes in the background, creating a record that could be held against me.

"Where were you?"

"Are you hurt?"

"What have they done to you?"

Who does my father think is *they*, I wonder but do not ask. What has he imagined has been happening to me for all those months?

With intolerable uncertainty, people are driven to find answers. Even when tolerable, uncertainty wears you down, until any answer is better than none.

"I was cold," I say flatly.

I offer solitary sensations, not a flurry of facts. Sensations like feelings need little explanation.

"It was dark."

My stomach heaves, and I taste bile as I jump up and run to the bathroom. My reflection in the vanity mirror looks knowingly back at me. I miss being Nathan.

Fixed though the moment is, moving inexorably with linear time, this reality of being home also spins on an axle of chaos. I let my mind drift and imagine finding solace among trans-dimensional beings I have encountered, who seem to have the godlike power to exist and not exist simultaneously. Though they rarely meddle in the mundanity our world has to offer, my actions of disruption and change have brought them ever closer to me. Is it their time shell that brings me to this moment? Have their ancient powers eroded the barriers that separate—cosmic silverfish chewing away at the pages of creation?

Or have I simply walked across a desert of illusions and self-deceptions like so many wandering monks before me, and come out on the other side, changed and yet the same?

The figure in the mirror beckons to me then, offering to trade places. I see my escape. Clumsily, almost childlike, I feel I'm crawling, drawn to the figure, drawn through an aperture to a landscape—an ocean where the waters are calmer. Seconds pass that appear timeless. We merge: the Steven in my dad's house, the Steven lost on the lake, and the Nathan who walked off the lake. I once again feel in command. We are together.

The front door of the house jars open, and I hear my mother call out for her child. Luckily, I'm on the usual side of the mirror—my face a simple reflection.

"Steven?"

"Steven, are you here?"

"Where is my boy?"

"Where is my baby boy?"

"There's my cookie monster!"

Unlike other loves, I muse, parental love endures.

Thankfully, I've made my way back through the mirror, back into the singularity of the everyday, and I meet her in the hallway. With minimal awareness of the colliding timelines between us, she urgently runs to me, arms outstretched. She has aged terribly. I can see that right away. Her eyes are dulled by grief and sorrow. Her touch, comforting and tainted by pain, sets my skin alight. I want to cry, to ask forgiveness, but detachment and the need for control will not allow it.

Instead, I follow my mother wordlessly back into the living room where the others wait. I tremble as if my body is no more substantial than a leaf in a windstorm.

They all come, some eventually, others repeatedly. My father, Aunt June, my brother John, and my sister Karen. My grandmother. And the reporters, of course.

In those early hours my mother barely lets go of me, and then she does for what seems to be days, though she stands right next to me. She leads me back to the sofa, cooing in a voice I have not heard since childhood. She asks the same questions—where have you been all this time, what happened on the lake?

At first, I don't answer.

I recall the integrated figure in the bathroom mirror—myself yet not myself, clouded by apertures to the unknowable, that somehow strengthens me. I can stumble past the abstractions and vagaries that served me earlier. My mother—not to mention the vulture press—demands more.

"I remember leaving my skis and backpack not far from the shore and walking out on the ice," I begin. "I was cold and lost my sense of direction. I couldn't find my stuff, and I kept walking."

I tell her, everyone, I have no memory of anything after that. I return over and over to the feeling of freezing, feeling colder than I'd ever been. And then opening my eyes in the field near Pittsfield. "I bought a newspaper and discovered it was May."

In a way, this is true. The Lake Michigan of this world is the last thing that the Steven back on the ice knew.

My mother's eyes, dull though they are, narrow. Behind them, I can see her thoughts gathering like storm clouds. As I expect of her, she is unraveling my story web as fast as I can weave it. I fill the spaces. I tell her about the maps in my backpack for cities like Reno, Chicago, and San Francisco. I wave at my T-shirt, which advertised a marathon in Wisconsin. My worn running shoes. "It appears I've been doing a lot of traveling," I offer.

I am glad I have buried the journals. She would know somehow if they were in the room.

"I hired a detective to look for you," she says. I pretend to be surprised.

"I want you to talk to him." I nod, make no commitment.

"I may make a report to the FBI," she states. I think my hand twitches at this. She does not miss the motion. My mother is a sharp woman, and my disappearance has put her through hell.

"There's also a deputy who was involved in the search for you. He told me he wants to talk to you if you turn up."

I nod again. I require more time to reflect on what to say. Not to decide which memories are true, of course, because in different realities and multiverses, all of the stories have happened. Steven has gone into the ice of Lake Michigan, and he hadn't. I am still in the mirror with Nathan, and I am also in this room.

Which histories can I bring here to this universe, here with my family? What realities to reveal, and what to leave as other? Probably none. For most people, it's fine to watch alternative dimensions and realities on TV, in movies, or in fantasy and sci-fi books. In those contexts, the everyday is suspended, but the reality of the viewers is not undone. However, if these aspects did become real, the audience's sense of certainty in a predictable, stable world would surely be upended, threatened.

What would my mom or dad do if they were in another dimension or reality? Wouldn't they be terribly scared? Wouldn't they fling their fears like mud to stick onto whatever was encountered, transforming the encounters into hellish landscapes or flying saucers filled with devils, monsters, and aliens, all out to harm them?

On further reflection, I think I'll keep this all to myself. Everything has been in my control, all along. For the time being, I have to believe that. Though unconditional acceptance and love by my family is emotionally overwhelming, I need to remain disciplined.

Chapter 3

A FLEXIBLE SENSE OF REALITY

The mission can only manifest and realize its wildest schemes through the utmost perseverance, dedication, and personal sacrifice. Otherwise forget it. You remain inconsequential idealists, romantics, and fanciful mystics. Impeccability implies enduring and vigilant watchfulness, a penultimate willingness to endure present and subjective hardships, a concern which leaves nothing to chance and wishful thinking, a thoroughness, and total abandonment.

—From the Nexalistic Revolutionary Front (NRF)
Documents by Nathan T. Stanfield (NTS)
a.k.a. Steven Kubacki, 1978

"Why don't I get the fuck out of here?"

On a warm Saturday in September, five months before my disappearance, Walter Smith and I are walking through the quaint streets of Holland, Michigan, deep in discussion as always. Our bodies are satiated with chocolate shakes from the student union—the kind made with real milk and ice cream, unlike the shakes down the road at Burger King made with chemicals. Our minds, however, are moving as fast as always.

We wind through one of the many parks that dot the town. Holland's annual Tulip Festival drew thousands of Dutch-flower-obsessed tourists every spring, but by fall, the carefully manicured tulip beds of Centennial Park are empty. They are now bare mounds of dirt in the shape of crosses, windmills, and stars that look like freshly covered graves without the stones.

As we pass the park's small pond, its stubby phallic fountain dry and covered with weeds, I say it. "Maybe I should just disappear."

"Why not just finish the year. Then do what you want," Walter suggests.

I know he ignored the last statement on purpose. Perhaps he thinks it is a bad idea. Perhaps he is trying to egg me on. Walter is adept at bringing out my radical side.

"But you know, I won't be able to do what I want to," I counter. "After college, I'll find some worthless job or attend graduate school. Then get married, become respectable, have kids, buy a house." I stop, gesture to the routine world around us. "Every year, every month, it gets harder to break out of the trap that dooms me to middle-class anonymity. Just like my father, who is like his father, involved in futile pursuits they have little control over, never knowing why; swept along, fumbling, but in the end accepting their lots."

"A world smug in the drama of its mediocrity," sings Walter.

I add, "In the park that manicured all life."

But as we walk farther, new words arise inside of me.

"I have to get out before it's too late."

"I must disappear."

"Soon."

In linguistics, language can have a performative function. An utterance such as "You are now husband and wife" can set into motion not only a new future, but a change in who you are, your identity. Did I set things in motion that day? Once said, my words could not be unsaid. A kind of incantation?

* * *

There are many places that I could point to and say, "This is where the story of the disappearance actually begins." None of them are on the ice of Lake Michigan in 1978. To comprehend what happened there, how time cracked open and Steven Kubacki disappeared for fifteen months, there are other things you need to know. The conversation in the park with Walter is one of them. But the true journey began almost a decade before that, in my childhood bedroom in South Deerfield, Massachusetts.

Because there would have been no disappearance without a past to pave the way, no discovery of Nexalism, no conspiracy, no founding of the NRF (the Nexalistic Revolutionary Front), and no multiverse revelations.

I was an unusually bright student, a precociously curious boy with a superior intelligence that confounded my working-class family. My test scores were off the charts, but at times I couldn't control my behavior and had to rebel. In elementary school, during Music Appreciation class, I flooded all the toilets in the basement. When my parents asked me why, I claimed boredom. I knew that they could never understand the truth—that I was filled with a sense of otherness. I had a thirst for heightened sensations: intellectual, physical, and emotional.

Nothing felt terribly real in elementary school, nothing usually mattered there. But I did like the challenge of memorizing pages and pages of facts in American History and getting them all correct on tests. High up on nearby Sugarloaf Mountain, I crashed into a tree head-first lying on a toboggan going down a luge run I'd built on snow-laden trails, resulting in crutches for a month. In late seventh grade, I fell in love with Cynthia, both of us believing I was dying of cancer because of bumps on private parts of my body, only to find out later they were the start of hair follicles in puberty. No, we didn't have sex.

Eventually, and perhaps just to get rid of me, a guidance counselor at Frontier Junior High School helped me get a scholarship to the prestigious Deerfield Academy, an elite school for those with wealth and privilege. Founded in 1797, Deerfield remains to this day one of the oldest college preparatory schools in the United States, renowned as much for its exclusivity as its academic excellence. There, I found academic exceptionalism flourishes as it perpetuates the procession of the powerful to their entitlements.

As the son of a factory worker, not surprisingly, I did not fit in.

Of course, by then I knew that I did not fit in anywhere, ever, but my adolescence at Deerfield was particularly harsh. My classmates were all from wealthy, prominent families. Their lives were mapped out like constellations. All they had to do was connect the dots and they would have great careers, power, money. I was different; I was alone. I had no map to success. While they jetted off to glamorous second and third homes and European tours, I had to work every summer to earn money for clothes and books. My first job, at thirteen, was picking tent tobacco in sometimes 110-degree heat, six days a week. The only perk was that the nicotine juice from the leaves soaked into my hands and gave me quite a rush. My friends and I sang silly songs as we moved up and down the rows of tobacco. I was slugged once by an older boy, Zack, from a nearby summer camp for the delinquent, without a reason. Later, my undercut leveled his friend Blum, and Zack threatened to kill me, but they didn't return. For those people at Deerfield, I might as well have been an alien from another planet.

I often reacted to the feeling of otherness by being even more "other." When all of the boys were growing their hair in tenth grade, I got a crew cut. I resented the teachers, who I thought looked down on me, and skipped classes in eleventh grade to spend time in the library, reading whatever caught my interest. I had no guidance from my family or teachers—nothing resembling mentorship to help me cope or find my way. I kept pushing people away for one reason or another: too boring, too stupid, too risk-averse. They all meant well, but no one seemed to have a purposeful understanding of their lives that I could make sense of. Why did they do what they did? They lived on automatic pilot.

At the end of my junior year, I had skipped so many classes that I was on the verge of being expelled. At my parents' insistence, I rallied in the final weeks of the semester, taking every make-up test available and writing essay after essay to get extra credit. I played the part of the good boy.

At the last minute, the school administrators had a change of heart and sent a letter offering me one last chance and a place in the senior class.

My parents, not surprisingly, celebrated my imminent return to the land of prestige and power; they had never understood why I was so unhappy there. But I retreated to my bedroom full of doubts.

I did not want to return to Deerfield, did not want to reenter a race I stood no chance of winning. I could already see that the Academy was an assembly line that stamped out tin figures of privilege, a machine that chewed up and spat out anything not fitting the approved mold.

And I was not willing to fit anyone's mold. I was not willing to be a part of the system. But I was. How could anyone not be part of some system?

What was the alternative, though? To leave the money and the attitudes behind and finish my education at the regional high school, which would likely put me on the track of those like my father, who squandered his energy and mental faculties in a factory making tires? The mere thought of such a future sent my sensitive mind spiraling into an alternate reality future, where I envisioned myself reduced to drugs and delinquency.

I paced like a caged animal, hopelessly trapped in a trajectory of banal absurdity that resembled Sartre's *No Exit* and Becket's *Waiting for Godot*. I would have preferred a Greek tragedy—a meaningful death in defiance of the gods, but those were reserved for the powerful, beautiful, or rich. Even if I graduated from Deerfield, the best I could hope for was more of the same. I would always be the poor kid trying to fit in, the smart kid not content with the status quo. I didn't want to be defined like that. I was capable of more and felt driven to be more.

As I mused, my eyes fell on a long-forgotten novel collecting dust on a bookshelf in the library, and in that instant, the other realities slipped away, and I found myself in a brighter realm.

No, the book wasn't *One Hundred Years of Solitude* or *Zen and the Art of Motorcycle Maintenance*. Nothing so predictably profound or world changing. It was, in fact, an almost forgotten 1950s science fiction story called *The Voyage of the Space Beagle* by A. E. van Vogt.

There, right in front of me, was the answer. Nexalism.

Nexalism was "applied whole-ism," according to the novel's main character, a young and precociously curious man named Grosvenor. In the book, Grosvenor uses his power of combining and synthesizing multiple fields of knowledge—multiple realities and narratives—to resolve complex problems and save his spaceship. While his crewmates repeatedly fail to defeat aliens and enemies with their narrow fields of study, Grosvenor's Nexalist training allows him to combine all that is useful, rather than adhere to the limitations and requirements of one system of thought, scientific or otherwise.

There was my answer. A man of many systems could not be beholden to the limitations or expectations of any one of them. A Nexalist would be free to make his own path, with nothing to inexorably control his destiny or rob him of choice.

I became a Nexalist that day, converting a way of reasoning from the unreal world of literature to the actual world, where, for the time being, I was a member of one.

Three weeks later, I returned to the sprawling Deerfield campus with new perspectives. Rather than give in to the lesser impulses of my rebellious nature, I used them to my advantage. I wanted to get at the methodologies and assumptions that guided thought and action, and by so doing, apply myself to mastering as many different systems as possible.

I went from failing my classes to excelling in them, because my purpose was no longer to simply submit or rebel against the expectations of others or the corrupt institutions they supported. I started to read more widely—Freud, Jung, quantum theory, Native American shamanism, and of course, plenty of science fiction. I became fascinated with Zen Buddhism, which I found intellectually rigorous in a way that went beyond the confines of rationality. In Zen's acceptance of life's contradictions, I could momentarily experience a kind of transcendence of those contradictions, both banal and profound. But most often, I practiced meditation and mindfulness as a way to escape my impatience and loneliness—to feel a connection with existence and not be alone, fleeting as that feeling always was.

I also became an activist. Fueled by Erich Fromm's condemnations of authoritarian value systems, I protested during the Academy's mock 1972 Democratic Convention, taking the stage with a fellow student to demand the legalization of all drugs and significant amendments to the Constitution. It didn't work, of course, but despite my anxiety, I discovered the power of my own voice.

Up to that point, I had found it difficult to speak before an audience. As a sophomore, I developed a stutter, the result of becoming so self-conscious and overly self-aware as a teenager that I couldn't trust anything I had to say. I wasn't shy by any means, but I did feel painfully judged by groups of people.

But I did not just wallow in my otherness. I filled journals with all the ways I'd save the world from hate and stupidity. To be honest, most of what I wrote was immature and even lame, and most of the time I was still a morose and sullen teenager. But there were seeds that later sprouted ideas. One phrase stands out: "Only action and total self-sacrifice can improve the plight of our species."

* * *

Everyone has a compulsion to immerse himself
in flames
To transform into steam
and disperse
and give up
I have collected this water
and have sprinkled it
to nourish
the Godless

—From the Nexalistic Revolutionary Front (NRF)
Documents by Nathan T. Stanfield (NTS)
a.k.a. Steven Kubacki, 1978

* * *

As my senior year blossomed into spring, admissions officers from Ivy League institutions descended on Deerfield in droves, hoping to snare its wealthy students with promises of power and advancement.

I found the entire college recruitment process totally bizarre. The application forms were tens of pages long. They wanted to know my favorite color, what kind of music my parents listened to, whether I preferred fruit juice or soda. Just another sign of a broken system, to my mind.

One afternoon, I escaped from the administration building and the college recruiters, longing for fresh air. But a spring storm was pelting the lawn with hail-sized raindrops, so I ducked into the library instead. As I wandered the familiar stacks, thumbing old favorites and potential new conquests alike, I realized that something was plastered to the bottom of my shoe, stuck there by rainwater.

It was an application form for Hope College in Michigan, a school I'd never heard of. What caught my attention was that the entire form was just two pages long, front and back. Then, whether due to some kind of screwup or because Hope wasn't on the same level as the other recruiting schools, I discovered that Hope's admissions officer had been sent to the library rather than the student hall. He saw me looking at the application and struck up a conversation. He described the school and the surrounding area, and something about it registered with me. I liked the idea of the lake—of a water wilderness—and Hope's reputation for getting students into medical school. At the time, I was considering medicine.

I applied right then and there and was soon offered nearly a full scholarship and federal student loans. I never bothered applying anywhere else.

At first, it seemed like a good choice. I arrived as a freshman in 1972, looking for a rebirth. Nearly 800 miles of land and water insulated me from my fracturing family, from the alienating politics of Deerfield, from my lackluster friends.

Inspired by possibility and freedom, I took to college like an artist to a new medium. My intermittent stutter disappeared entirely. I drank cheap beer with my fellow pre-med students in the Pine Grove and at Skiles Tavern, and I explored the woods and water. I maxed out my limit at the library, loading my nightstand with books on math, chemistry, physics, and biology. I wondered; if I could master all the sciences, maybe I could discover a way to be immortal. Yes, that was a fantasy, but one of my jobs as a Nexalist was to determine how a fantasy could become a reality. I thought if I could live long enough, perhaps I could gain a knowledge and wisdom that could be indispensable. To that I critically wrote:

Invincible individuals
invariably
imagine
an
illusionary
immortality

It didn't take long, however, to discover that I still didn't fit in with the academic stairway to established success (the antithesis of Led Zeppelin's "Stairway to Heaven"). I hadn't done enough research to realize that Hope College had been founded as a Christian institution, based on the theology and conservative ideology of the Dutch Reformed Church. They'd required religious classes until just a year or two before I arrived, and the overall feeling on campus was still highly traditional.

Tradition didn't suit me. I was still a rebel, a Nexalist determined to break the molds. I fashioned a harness out of rope and rappelled from my fourth-floor dormitory window rather than using the stairs. I broke into the chapel and brought women there to make out in front of the altar. While in a chemistry research lab, I cooked a hot dog in a mass spectrometer, then wrote a poem to reflect on it.

S is for Steven

Searching for

a sacred singularity

in the sensible sea

of scholarly stones

I didn't care about the possibility of punishment when it came to breaking the rules. Consequences implied a shared experience, repercussions for breaking established rules. But if you don't belong—if you're not part of that shared construct—why worry about the rules at all? It's the one benefit to being the *other*: other people's rules and systems didn't apply to me. As I reflect now, this kind of arrogance—a disregarding of the rules—is still part of me for good and ill.

* * *

My roommate at the time, a guy named Tom, introduced me to LSD in the spring of our freshman year. I'd been reading a lot about transcendental experiences at that point, and I'd always been able to detach myself from the obvious reality around me—what we call dissociation today—but my first experience with LSD was life-changing, and so were my thoughts:

I have never seen the color red. Not like this, free of shadow. This is purity. All of the colors and the absence of color...darkness itself, free of shadow!

My eyes—my mind—had edited out and suppressed the true expanse of the universe. But no more. Never again.

Tom and I walk the campus for minutes, hours, decades. We are balanced on the edge of infinity. We talk about nothing, everything, about streams of woven air, and the grains of sand along the walkways. We are silent. The silence hears us. It invites us into it, where the sounds around improvise the day's melody like a jazz ensemble.

When the sky darkens, lamps adorn the way to buildings, places, and opaque distant worlds. The lamps become suns with thousands of insects orbiting them like asteroids and planets. The blackness of space overhead is alive. You can hear it breathe.

There is a man under a lamp, a Christian proselytizing and holding a Bible. He is devoid of the color red, or of any color. The energy that rains from the cosmos on everything else avoids his robotic gestures and words. I am sad. He is inert, encased, invertebrate, a puppet. Something inhuman is pulling his strings.

I turn to Tom. "I hope that never happens to me."

* * *

When I went back to Massachusetts that summer, I spent as much time as possible outdoors. My parents had divorced while I was away at Hope, and my mother had quickly remarried a technician from the University of Massachusetts named Harry Pegg.

I didn't blame my mother for the split—my father was a difficult man who today would be diagnosed as bipolar. He would manically clean or start an unnecessary yard project at five in the morning, waking everyone in the house and demanding our help, while berating us for not being as smart as him. Sometimes he railed for hours about how we were against him, and on many nights, he self-medicated with heavy drinking and a constant stream of mindless TV sitcoms: *Hogan's Heroes*, *Gilligan's Island*, *Columbo*, *All in the*

Family—though I must admit, I liked them too. He picked fights with my mother on a regular basis. Although my father was also generous and tried his clumsy and uninformed best to be attentive and help with chores, my mother had had enough. While he and I had many loud arguments mostly about nothing, my father would help in anyway he could and always had my back.

After a year of freedom and independence, it chafed me to live with Harry, who struck me as an autocrat of the worst kind. He liked order and control—or at least the illusion of it. We didn't see eye to eye on anything, and there was always an undercurrent of hostility between us. Beneath his taciturn forbearance, he was always judging. In Michigan, my mind was expanded by experiences I could not have imagined, and I could do whatever I wanted: experiment with drugs, discuss ideas passionately and deeply with my professors and friends, chase girls, talk about Buckminster Fuller, space exploration, corporate malfeasance, existentialism, and poetry. I wasn't okay with someone setting a curfew for me—I never had one growing up—out of some sad power trip.

To get away, I climbed the crumbly rock faces of Mount Sugarloaf, an outcropping the local Algonquin tribe taught was the bones of a giant god, and spent one memorable night on Mount Washington, a notoriously dangerous peak in New Hampshire. Along with my childhood friend Charles—the one who a few years later would travel to Michigan to help search for me on the ice—I climbed it at night, took some acid, and built a makeshift tent. I could literally feel the cosmic winds blowing through me. I belonged there. Or rather, I belonged in that state of mind.

As banks of fog churn in the valley below the mountain, the universe becomes a whirling mandala of effervescent colors, and I eat

them, as if ingesting light is like breathing in air. With my hand I reach out to the stars and pluck out new colors, placing them in my mouth and consuming them. The more I eat, the more my body takes on their shifting shades. I become a palette of purple, then green, then electric blue—all the colors I've now seen in telescope pictures of distant nebula and galaxies. I understand now the fundamental truth of what Sagan said: "We're made of star stuff."

I'd always been gifted with a flexible sense of what reality could be, but after taking LSD, I was at a level that defied linguistic expression. Like the endless trees in a vast forest, the world at large seemed full of endless possibilities. Things made more sense to me under the stars, and when in some other dimension, I could sample their existence.

As the night winds on and the fog banks continue to encircle the mountain, I ascend higher and higher into some kind of cosmic mind. I remember that the Buddha was sometimes depicted in different colors, too. The world falls away beneath me; first the mountaintop, then the Earth itself. I am surrounded by something Other—not human, at least. These are fifth-dimensional beings, or perhaps something higher, moving in parabolic waves. I can feel them downloading information from me, to me, from other timelines and realities. I am formless, connected to the planets, rotating with stars, the universe—I am in a hall of mirrors, within which infinite realities contain infinite versions of myself, but thankfully mostly not myself. It would be a burden and far too human-centric otherwise.

I see someone who looks like me, and I recognize it as a higher version of myself. This other me has a goatee, and he stands in a glass room in front of countless levers. I somehow know that if my goatee self pulls on a lever, my destiny could change. One lever—the one that

would make me a doctor—has not been pulled, but others already have been.

The next morning, on the hike down, I had the overwhelming feeling that I had not returned to the right reality. The higher dimensional Steven had somehow interfered with my return, causing me to land in another Steven Kubacki's body, displacing yesterday's me in the process.

My otherness took on new significance. I had literally become an interloper from another reality, out of step with this one.

"I envision the cosmos to be composed of an infinite number of realities," I wrote in my journal. "God exists and does not exist. I am already a prophet, poet, drunkard, thief, and dishwasher. I wonder if the darkness is the light before the dawn, a creativity in shadow, emergent selves I have yet to meet."

When I returned to Hope that fall, I had not forgotten about the goateed me with the levers. I quit the hard sciences, much to my mother's dismay, and turned to poetry, German, and philosophy. As I surrounded myself with writers and artists, Tom and I took to hanging out in bars at night and sleeping during the day. I tried to become an alcoholic, because that's what poets and writers do, but I couldn't find any truth in drunkenness, nor any peace—only boredom.

Eternally dead, what is there to lose? Damned and forsaken, we abandon history to scholars. Unconcerned with the vicissitudes of permanence and personal failure, time is discarded, actions are powerful, footsteps — light and gentle.

—From the Nexalistic Revolutionary Front (NRF)
documents by Nathan T. Stanfield (NTS)
a.k.a. Steven Kubacki, 1978

Chapter 4
THE ORIGINS OF THE NRF

The nice thing about thinking, fantasizing, and making up conversations and scenarios in your mind is that you don't need to act on them. People have all kinds of horrific thoughts and imaginings but don't act on them. Our world wouldn't be able to function otherwise. Thinking, planning, scheming, plotting, writing, art, and practicing whatever's in your head, these are all inhibitory processes that make us the successful species we are.

—Letter sent from Nathan T. Stanfield to Paul Morrison, 1978

Along with the light of discovery, though, comes darkness.

In our sophomore year, Tom and I moved into an old house off campus where we held weekly meetings. Attendees wore hooded robes, discussed Tolkien, and puffed on long stem clay pipes. These are some of my favorite memories of my time as a college student.

There was something dark in that house, though—a presence that wasn't new to me.

I was born with what everyone back then, even medical professionals, called a "lazy eye." I had corrective surgery on it when I was four years old, which restored my vision beautifully, but something about the experience brought unexpected side effects. My awareness of other realms, along with my ability to move into other states of consciousness, was heightened from that point right up to the present day.

I was in the hospital often as a kid, with fevers, a double hernia, appendicitis, tonsillitis, and pneumonia. A lot of people don't realize that suffering can be an act of expansion. To endure suffering, you need to grow and expand out of it. In my case, this meant opening doorways that allowed me to escape my situation. But doors go both ways.

Sometimes, when I was alone and in pain, I could see my brother Michael, who had died as an infant. He was always in the company of a dark, shapeless presence. At first, I thought I was simply having bad dreams. But then I stopped seeing Michael and the dark presence came alone, filling me with dread and despair. Nightmares of trauma and horror sometimes lingered into my waking hours, and at times strange visions from another person's life came and went like migraines.

By the time I was a teenager, I suspected there was more to what was happening than normal dreams. This wasn't something that was all in my head. I began to see the dark presence as a parasite, something that had anchored itself to me during those first six weeks of life when my mother had been too ill to hold me. But of course, this was all happening in the early 1970s. People didn't talk about other realms and realities the way they do now. Pain was something to be covered up, not explored. And my parents weren't particularly attuned to me. They didn't understand me, though they were devoted. So, despite my signs of trouble, there were no conversations, no counseling or therapy.

Instead, I turned to books to understand what was happening. I read about the concept of hungry ghosts drawn from Buddhism, and the evil spirit called the Wendigo, a local Algonquian legend. I read about astral projection and lucid dreaming, and how medieval magicians used to trap spirits to cast them out. That proved to be a particularly useful tool for someone like me.

The next time the dark presence came for me, I was ready.

I have made a box of light in my dream. This is lucid dreaming, a skill that's taken me months to master, but now will possibly save me.

The box rests in my hands as I wait, asleep but aware, ready.

When the dark presence comes, I pounce first. I have power it does not know about, power I have kept hidden until now, a power of light. I use it to capture the presence, to force its darkness into the box of light. Close it, seal it, so escape from it is not possible.

And it worked. But the dark presence is powerful. It's been with me since my first breath and will remain for many years to come. I am inexperienced in shamanic practices.

The darkness bursts out of the box and attacks me, filling me with dread. It knows I am losing and I know it is winning. I awake myself and manage to fall out of my bed. I crawl slowly to the bedroom door. It takes all my strength to pull the door open, to let the light from the hallway stream into the room.

The darkness flees. My trap has frightened it. The presence does not return for a while.

* * *

The presence in the house in Holland felt similar to what I'd known in Massachusetts. One night, I had a dream where the darkness entered my room in the basement of the house. Its heaviness filled me, and I sank through the concrete of the floor, and then through the Earth, until I was in another dimension. I woke up terrified, still feeling the crushing weight of the Earth. But it wasn't the familiar Earth of which I was part. It was the darkness. The darkness was pressing the Earth against me.

The next day, I used a shamanic trick that I'd read about to energize a bunch of stuffed animals, filling them with protective power and then placing them all around the room. The presence never entered my room again.

Instead, it shifted its attention to Tom. My roommate started having nightmares and losing sleep. His girlfriend—a French exchange student—complained and argued with him about the strange things happening in the house. It got so bad that she broke up with him and moved back to France.

Tom was devastated, and a pall of negativity settled over the house. Our weekly Tolkien discussions ceased, and he sank into self-pity. I knew that he was in a bad spot, but I was floored to come home one day to find him packing his bags. He said he was leaving for France to try to win his girlfriend back. He told me I could sell his belongings if it was a problem. I knew he was being sarcastic, but I felt disappointed and sick of his drama, and so that's what I did. I sold, for $30, his Underwood typewriter and his two-volume set of the Oxford Dictionary.

That didn't go over well when he got back a few weeks later, but I didn't care. Tom and I were already drifting apart, and I felt he was just keeping me around for his own amusement, using my intelligence, wildness, and even my darkness to impress and amuse his friends.

* * *

One benefit of my falling out with Tom was that it made it easier for me to pack my own bags. I'd landed a scholarship to study abroad for my junior year at the University of Freiburg in Germany, a classic bastion of knowledge and learning since the Renaissance.

It was my first trip overseas, and I was immediately infatuated with Europe and Europeans. One of my early classes was in parapsychology; it was taught by Eberhard Bauer, who was famous for investigating cases of paranormal and supernatural activity. It was the first time I'd ever heard academic lectures on the links between poltergeists and the untapped power of the human mind. Bauer believed there was a human explanation for most of what seemed inexplicable, and that people could warp and distort the fabric of time. I sometimes wondered what he would think about my dark presence—I suppose he would have seen it either as a psychological manifestation created by my inner turmoil or as an unknown scientific phenomenon, like a time traveler or an extraterrestrial. But I never asked him.

My first real friend in Europe was Richard Turner, an American with a Southern drawl who I met in a bar in Paris, where he attended the Sorbonne. Richard came from a wealthy family and was generous by default, as quick with his wallet as with his wit. Over time, I saw there was a neediness to his generosity, in a way both charming and a bit manipulative. He liked to feel important.

In between academic quarters, when Richard invited me on a grand tour of Europe, I couldn't say no, and met him in Strasbourg. We hitched rides through Strasbourg to Lyon, then down south to Marseilles. We camped with a gang of anarchists and talked late into the night about everything from Martin Luther King to Molotov cocktails. When we reached Barcelona, we slept among the city's homeless, then bought wine and drank it at a table by the side of the road. At one point,

I split off from Richard to go to Rome with a woman named Melanie. We hitchhiked through twenty-mile-long tunnels under mountains in Switzerland and even went to Mass at the Vatican with Pope Paul VI. I took communion in Rome, though I'd never been a practicing Catholic. Why not enlist Jesus, I thought. I needed all the spiritual energy I could get.

That was a year of reckless and exhilarating adventure, testing all of the boundaries and fearing nothing. At one point in Switzerland, Richard and I were picked up by a van full of Scientologists who invited us back to their residence. Before Richard could say no, I agreed.

Before long, we found ourselves separated in windowless white rooms. There was a strange white machine in the corner, and after about an hour, a team of people who introduced themselves as "auditors" came in. They were all wearing white, and even their glasses were identical. I agreed to let them hook me up to the machine and ask me questions, both personal and trivial.

I'd just spent a semester studying Jungian psychology, so I decided to toy with the cultists. I answered every question in a way that directly contradicted the last, probably sending the machines into histrionics. Dials spun, red lights flashed, and a printer in the corner of the room spat out coded sheets of paper.

The kindly auditors informed me that I was the unwitting host of some fifty alien souls and offered to purge the parasites for a small fee. I just smiled and shook my head at them, saying that the aliens had chosen me for a reason, to be the savior of mankind.

They threw me out so fast my head spun. Richard was already outside waiting, ready to laugh about the whole experience. But a small part of me left the Scientologists wondering whether those strange machines had been more accurate than I wanted to acknowledge. Was something living within me?

* * *

Returning to Hope after a year at Freiburg, I felt energized, determined to begin a new chapter of my life. Once again, I transferred majors, this time to political science.

The optimism didn't last. I found the American classrooms disengaged and mentally undisciplined compared to the blunt, unflinching method of German political discourse. Complex topics like inner-city segregation or the fall of Saigon were reduced to pill-sized blurbs meant for quick consumption. I decided that my professors were unconcerned with pushing the political envelope, focusing instead on personalities of popular figures like then-Governor Ronald Reagan. They showed no interest in examining the systems and algorithms that had propelled these "great men" into power, and even less in the negative outcomes wrought by their leadership.

It was a perfect example of the Culture Industry, a term coined by Theodor Adorno and Max Horkheimer that my friends and I threw around a lot in those years. My classmates had exchanged their outrage for mass-manufactured films, fashion, music, and magazines. They had let themselves be tricked into subservience, becoming just another generation of bovine consumers. Marx said the opium of the people was religion, which distracted the masses from their true economic and political self-interests. Now consumption and commodification are the opium of the people, co-opting them so that the powerful can manipulate and control them with ease.

As the Nexalist I was, I didn't hesitate to articulate to my fellow students my perspectives on their adherence to a master-slave dynamic, as described by Nietzsche. Unsurprisingly, my classmates didn't like being compared to cattle. Tom was no longer speaking to me, and Richard was far away in Atlanta. I would have been a total outcast, except that I discovered the one person who shared my outrage.

I met James Courtier in a political science class and immediately thought that he seemed refined and good-looking. He came up to me after a particularly heated argument with the professor and offered to buy me a beer after class. I could tell right away he was different.

Over several rounds of the only imported beer on tap, I learned that James was a dual Belgian-American citizen, raised mostly overseas. He clearly came from wealth, but he wasn't driven by it—or at least didn't seem to be at the time.

I told him about my recent overseas adventures, and he listened as no one else had. I found him well-read, adventurous, wary of authority, politically radical, and conscious of the wider world. He wasn't afraid of my wild side or jealous of my intellect like Tom. In fact, he came across as even more excited than me about taking risks and challenging the status quo.

Overnight, we became almost inseparable. When we weren't together on campus, we were traveling, hitchhiking wherever the wind took us.

We discussed if pure democracy was possible or if it would eventually lapse into anarchy. We harped on the Culture Industry, critiquing how frustrating it was that the systems could co-opt all of our ideas, hopes, and dreams, repackaging and selling them back to us. We agreed that everything, even our very selves, had become a monetized product. All had been co-opted by the rich and powerful over time, including the so-called "countercultural movements" of the 1960s and revolutions and reforms like the American Revolution,

Roosevelt's New Deal, the Mexican Revolution, colonial uprisings and revolts, Martin Luther, New Age spiritualities, and even Joan of Arc from fifteenth-century France.

(None of this has changed, by the way. People still like to identify with change, reform, and revolution, but when it's packaged anew and sold back to them by the powers that be, the status quo isn't threatened or undone—not really. Change becomes a simulated, vicarious, as-if experience without much substantive action or self-sacrifice for the greater good. Most of us are too comfortable to let go of our houses and bank accounts. With access to TV, streaming content, sports, caffeine, drugs, and pornography, why would anyone risk a revolution, or even mobilize a union? And it's only gotten worse. Social media platforms appropriate our wants and interests and monetize them for their owners, all while creating the false appearance of community and connection.)

James and I saw ourselves as outsiders, anomalies, and standard deviations from the mean. We discussed how we could break the system, though not like Mao had done it in the Cultural Revolution, where the carnage was terribly high—with tens of millions killed—and it failed anyway. Was it better to immerse ourselves as spies and hope that when we rose to the top, we'd be able to change the system from within? That, we agreed, was an illusion—everyone who enters the system eventually becomes part of the system.

The last and probably most viable option, we concluded, was to become an outsider and create an alternative culture, politics, and economics.

Our friendship mostly waxed, and a few times it waned, as the relationships of young and passionate people are prone to do. But we were more than just best friends. We were vagabonds, travelers in both physical and metaphysical worlds.

Though James came from a wealthy family, somehow we were always broke. He and I rented an apartment in the attic of a local family who lived near the Hope College campus, but after a series of travels and adventures, we found ourselves short on rent but full of words and ideas. One afternoon, when I heard our landlady, Marge, climbing the stairs to the attic where we lived, I hastily opened a can of dog food, which many weeks before I had accidentally discovered in a corner of the huge attic. When Marge came in and saw what I was cooking on my little hot plate, she winced in shock.

"It's not so bad once you got used to it," I said, keeping a straight face. I reached down into an old bag of dry dog food that we'd also found, threw some kibbles in the air, and caught them with my mouth.

Marge immediately invited James and me to eat with her and her family, and she didn't ask about rent for several months.

Another thing that held James and me together was our disdain for Hope College, which we started calling *Hoax* College. One night, James and I climbed up into the rafters of the student union building during a packed assembly about radicalism. Patty Hearst had just been captured, and the Baader-Meinhof gang was stirring up trouble in Germany again. As the dean droned on and on about the dangers of radicalism, we hopped from beam to beam dozens of feet above everyone's heads—seemingly removed from all their bullshit. It reminded me of Tom Sawyer at his own funeral for some reason—like the dean was down there talking about me.

Perhaps that's when the story really starts, the moment in the rafters when I thought—what if we just dropped out? What if we just left—abandoned the system altogether?

***

Have you ever pictured reality as a bubble, floating on the surface of an ocean alongside countless other bubbles—other realities?

They'd all be separated by their individual membranes, but they would still be affected by the same tides, winds, and waves—that is, forces, events, and things outside and beyond them. Such forces would affect the individual realities of each bubble. They would shape the very histories of the bubbles in ways each bubble could not imagine.

So often, history is viewed as linear sequence of events, owing in large part to the actions of so-called "great men." When you read it written down, there is a rhyme to it, a story even. Great men accomplishing great things—empires, kingdoms—achieving all of it with almost omniscient clarity of thought in the moment. But do you really think Alexander the Great knew what he was doing when he set out to do it? Or Jesus Christ? No. History is largely chaos, influenced by the accumulative forces of the mundane and even trivial.

But there are also forces far beyond our understanding of reality, forces that are nearly incomprehensible. Like the wind and the waves beyond the bubble.

If we could somehow understand the non-ordinary aspects of reality—break free of our bubbles and see the whole picture, so to speak—we might be able to influence things as much as the wind and waves.

* * *

While I never hesitated to share my thoughts in any of my college classes, there was one class in particular, Theories of Political Science, that became a daily sparring match. While I personally liked the professor, Daniel Bart, I also considered him a wannabe intellectual and relished the opportunity to interrupt and challenge his well-rehearsed lectures. One time, I argued that Dr. Bart had not understood the radical materialism of Marx in respect to Hegel's idealistic dialectics and their anti-democratic motifs. I even had the gall to suggest that he read *The Wealth of Nations* and *The Theory of Moral Sentiments* by Adam Smith to critique *The Writings of YoungMarx*.

Bart saw my outbursts for what they were—youthful arrogance and a plea for guidance and direction. He attempted to take me under his wing, I can see now, but at the time, I resented the way he kept telling me what I was, who I was. I saw myself as a fountain of youth and Bob as an out-of-touch relic trying to use me to recapture his energy.

I went out of my way to fail Bart's class, but he wouldn't let it happen. He even invited me over for dinner at his house and implored me to put my intellect to better use. My fascination with revolution in political science, philosophy, and economics would get me nowhere good, he warned.

"Steven, my boy, if you want to join the elites, you need to step up and play the game," he told me, and then he gave me an ultimatum—either I behave in his class and stop turning it into a circus, or he would fail me and ensure I was tossed out of Hope to work in a factory forever.

He had me over a barrel, so I agreed to his terms and proposed a large research essay that would make up for all missing and future assignments. He let me pick the subject and the method of research, which is how I spent that semester, and many months that followed, working on a history and content analysis of my favorite philosophers, historians, mystics, and nonlinear thinkers.

In the end, what I produced was more of a book-length manifesto than a paper; I called it *The NonLinguistics of History*. James threw himself into helping with my research, even writing some of the paper, and became my principal sounding board and editor.

My aim had been to highlight the flawed ways in which we viewed and studied history when we talked only about great men accomplishing great things. I wanted to expose them all—even the outliers and so-called revolutionaries like Marcuse, Foucault, and even Adorno—as sellouts neutered by the system. I wanted to explore an alternative to the established narrative of history by great historiographers like Müller and Sorokin. My belief was that forces beyond our perceived reality had more to do with shaping our lives than we knew. Some were mundane and trivial, but there were also incomprehensible forces—forces that affected the entire multiverse. I concluded that none of it mattered as long as the status quo was maintained. The system wouldn't allow for such thinking to influence alternative ways of looking at reality. The hardest part of the research and writing was seeing where I fit into that system—a future of being marginalized in a career that served the entrenched powerful, with no ability to make real change.

By the time I finished writing *The NonLinguistics of History* in the spring of 1977, I was consumed with anger and dismay. But I was also caught up in a fervor, an uncanny faith that the universe somehow would come to my aid and guide me.

After my disappearance, the press and Hope College gossips had a field day with the idea that I'd been studying revolutions and countercultural ideas. In a way, they were right and should have been suspicious.

Though he failed as a mentor, Daniel Bart deserves my thanks. If he had not challenged me to explore and define what I believed, it's likely I never would have vanished that day on the lake.

* * *

Let us be mad.

Let us overturn the world

From dream to dreamlike reality

—From the Nexalistic Revolutionary Front (NRF)
Documents by Nathan T. Stanfield (NTS)
a.k.a. Steven Kubacki, 1978

* * *

It was during those heady times that James and I met Paul Morrison. I don't even remember the first time he entered our circle; he was simply there one day.

Paul was a theology student at Hope, but he wasn't the typical Reformed minister-in-training. Paul was a modern critical thinker, for one thing, and radically attuned to the ways that the messages of religion could be used to bring liberation and equality to the human race. He was willing to debate the existence of God in frank terms that I admired. He could read the early philosophers and mystics in their original Greek and Latin, and it was quickly apparent that he was far better trained in modern philosophy than I was.

James sometimes thought Paul was too dogmatic, but Paul and I had the greatest conversations. Instead of arguing about specific visions of God or higher powers, we focused on how philosophy could become a form of action or praxis to save humanity from stupidity. Paul was especially interested in how to improve authentic and collaborative communication instead of the usual manipulative and strategic forms of communication, which were focused not on understanding but on winning regardless of the cost and how it was achieved. Jürgen Habermas was his favorite in this regard.

In the fall of 1977, I found myself living with James in the attic of a large house just off the "Hoax" campus. We didn't have much money, but between us we'd amassed a huge collection of books, and our apartment was a maze of paper walls and hardcover corridors. James worked diligently on his economics degree, while I worked even harder to ignore my studies completely. My discontent with life and with school grew worse every year. The anger and jealousy I had carried since my school days wouldn't let me rest.

I found myself itching to get back at the status quo, so my friends and I set out on a campaign to terminate the Hope College student council. To me, the entire organization was nothing more than a den of lackeys to the administration, and so I publicly and repeatedly condemned their involvement, or lack thereof. With help from a friend who worked at the radio station, I recorded a series of attacks, urging my fellow students to *Not Vote* in the upcoming election. This, too, became an activity that was misunderstood when I disappeared, with newspapers reporting that I had made "anti-government" films.

The campaign created quite a ruckus on campus, and the administration, perhaps fearful that we might succeed, began their own counter-campaign. They set up voting tables in the school's cafeteria and pressured every student who walked through the doors to cast a ballot. In the end, that year's student council election saw the highest levels of participation in the college's history, and I saw again how ruthless those in power can be when threatened. They were not concerned with trying to reach an understanding with us—that is, authentic communication—but only in winning.

Increasingly disappointed by ordinary reality, I turned more and more to the reality of infinite possibilities and the potential for individual change. I took a couple more trips on LSD that shattered my notions of self, but I could not break out of this world. I always returned. The world had not changed. Still, hoping Nexalism could be the key, I devoured books on shamanism, non-ordinary realities, astrophysics, and Hermetic history—themes I would return to again and again throughout my life.

But all these efforts were not enough; I became disenchanted with them. Individual enlightenment and self-transformation weren't sufficient to change me or the world. I might be exploring myself, but the systems that governed still had me by the throat. Whatever notions of power and knowledge I had were vanquished by their enormity. I was nothing, I knew nothing. My future seemed like nothing but a horrific existence to endure.

And then I had that conversation with Walter Smith in the park.

"I have to get out before it's too late."

* * *

On a dreary October night in 1977, a few weeks after that conversation, I invited a small group of friends to the attic apartment for a game of Risk—the strategy game with the object of taking over the world. One by one, people made their excuses, including James. They were traveling or studying or going somewhere else. In the end, the only people who showed up that night were Walter and Paul.

I saw the meeting as something like fate, something archetypal or otherworldly that was moving chess pieces, of which this event was one. I'd been looking for a way to introduce my closest friends to a radical idea without frightening them. Fate chose the three of us, and we were never the same.

While we played the game, I told them a story, one that took the idea of risk and turned it toward revolution.

Long ago, long before anyone could remember—a three-headed dragon rose to take control of mankind. One head was called Empire, the other Church, and the last Coin. Together, they formed the pillars of a new civilization that took many names and many faces yet always remained the same.

Because the faces and the names kept changing, people eventually forgot about the dragon. They came to view each head as a thing unto itself, with each driven by an independent agenda. But in truth, the heads were no more independent from one another than a person's left arm is from their right.

The dragon manipulated and shaped the world to serve its interests. People were its food. From time to time, there would be a revolution—an empire would topple, a religion would be snuffed out. But nothing really changed. Despite revelations, declarations, proclamations, and wars that targeted one head or another, the dragon still lived and fed.

If someone really wanted to beat the dragon, I explained to my friends, they couldn't just lop off one head or another. They had to take all three simultaneously. And there was a way to do that wouldn't spill a single drop of blood. A man didn't need to fight the dragon to conquer it. In fact, that would never work.

A man had to *become* the dragon.

Walter saw right away where I was going with my little fable. He got this look in his eyes—part fearful, part excited—while I talked, but he didn't interject.

I delivered my pitch.

Richard, I reminded them, is on track to become a lawyer in Georgia, where his family has incredible political power. With his father's connections and money, it was only a matter of time before he transitioned into politics—or Empire.

I turned to Paul. "And you are on your way to seminary."

"Church," he whispers.

"A new kind of Christianity," I suggest.

"It's been on my mind for a long time," he affirms.

Walter doesn't wait for me to point out the obvious. "And I'm Coin," he says. Walter was studying business and finance at Calvin College, with an eye toward becoming the CEO of an international corporation and building a fortune to surpass that of his father, a wealthy real estate mogul.

We talk back and forth on the idea for the rest of the night, discussing the ins and outs of such an undertaking. It is easier to convince them than I had anticipated. No one points out how crazy it all is to think that a few college kids could change the world. I think it's because Walter and Paul feel like I do—angry and trapped by a system they don't want to support. They've grown up on the same diet of bullshit that praises greatness and significance, ignoring how prescribed those paths are: paths filled to the brim with the self-centered and self-serving, spiced with a scattering of the altruistic and progressive. In the end, they all leave intact the authoritarian and bureaucratic structures that rule us, including those in control.

I say again, "What I am offering is a chance to do something different—something truly significant."

Finally, Paul asks the obvious question. "And what part will you play in all of this? Is there a fourth head to the dragon?"

"There is no fourth head," I tell them. "But there is a body."

This is where my plan really takes off. The thing that would bind us all together in our cause has to be hidden beneath the surface. If the others are going to spend their lives working to achieve the highest levels of government and church and business, they would need someone to keep them unified and on mission. That is me. I will be the one to raise the army, start the war, if necessary. And I will do it all anonymously.

Which means Steven will have to die.

"It's outrageous," Walter argues, but he is smiling.

"It's exactly what we need to shake things up," I reply.

"Let's forget it. You know what happens when we begin to seriously consider these mad ideas of yours," Paul adds, "We end up doing them."

We sit in silence for a few minutes, each of us thinking. Then Walter's smile turns to laughter. "Okay, what's your plan?"

I am ready with my answer. "I fake my death. You'll supply me with a car and cash and send me to...I don't know, Mexico. That's your job. I'll live in a dojo, recruit fighters of the highest caliber, dedicated to a transcendent mission like monks. With no records, I'll be totally mobile so I can organize without harassment and prying from parents and friends—and police. I can't exist. Can't you see its simplicity?"

The four of us will be a conspiracy in its most classic sense—a small group of people joined together through deception in a secret cause. I knew that conspiracies only held together if there was something significant to hold them together, something that, if exposed, would create serious problems for everyone.

I was willing to become that bond and was sure that the way to do it was disappearing. This would cement us together to launch the first revolution of its kind. I would access the power necessary to transform the dragon's body. Together with the three heads, we would be formidable. We would change the world.

We couldn't become more significant than that.

* * *

Incompetence and indifference on a scale unpardonable leads me to conclude that without a doubt I must also liberate my actions and thoughts from their own immobility fashioned by my reliance and trust in others not so dedicated and persevering as myself, friends who by my permission and lack of foresight reduced me to their laziness. I must condemn them as fleas, cowards, counterrevolutionaries. Embarrassment, even though it was I in my need for power who created and allowed their establishment. In short, it's better to act alone and upon one's own wits than to unnecessarily compromise oneself for the sake of immediate gain.

—Letter from James to Steven, 1977

* * *

"Boom! Boom!" I declare, "You're all dead. We have won!"
Wait, I think, more are coming.
I worry, we won't have enough men. We may all have to die.
Now, we are losing, but we must hold out. Where are
the reinforcements?
Forty left. Me and my buddy are wounded. How can we win?

Yes, stand up our dead men. The enemy will think they're alive.
The enemy comes out shooting. But the bodies stay up. They can't believe it!
From behind the rocks, we shoot them all.

I shout, "We tricked them!"

They're all dead, their tanks destroyed. But one enemy appears—the last one. He wasn't so dumb. He hid behind a tank. He tries to shoot my buddy. I jump in front. I get hit in the heart.

"Bang!" My buddy shoots back. But it's too late. I die.

"You have saved us," he says, "We'll remember you!"

The battle is over. I separate the soldiers. Two hundred or more of the enemy, green; thirty or so of the good guys, grey. I hide the grey ones on the bookshelves, in the closet, and under the bed. The green ones are spread on the open floor. The enemy has lots of tanks and artillery. We have hand grenades and bazookas. We aren't a lot, but we're smarter. We're ready to fight and die.

—Steven, age six

Chapter 5

NATHAN T. STANFIELD

Shrill dreams stagger solemn
to unite in secret graves
I watch you whenever you happen to wander
pale in the institution of your philosophy

Establish
the truth through prevarication
Bring in the distorters of cognition
To assure the sensitive
that their daily slavery
is not repressive
But truly represents the joy of knowing
The mute whispers of fragmented consciousness

—From the Nexalistic Revolutionary Front (NRF)
Documents by Nathan T. Stanfield (NTS)
a.k.a. Steven Kubacki, 1978

Yes, I faked my own death in February 1978—at least, that is what I did *here*. On another plane of existence and in a different reality, I did disappear on that ice. I sometimes have clear flashes of memory of my body going through frozen water. Of floating in the sky, pulled forward by something above me. Of being swallowed by a spirit, perhaps the spirit of the lake itself. I remember things that seem impossible, given what happened after a me left the lake. Run-ins with death like I had—even the staged kind—are portals to other timelines, uniting us with our other multiverse selves.

But here in this realm, my decision to disappear was entirely my own and that of my co-conspirators. To accomplish my purpose, which was nothing less than becoming a revolutionary sowing seeds of unrest and disrupting the systems of oppression, I was certain I had to sever all ties to the life of Steven Kubacki; I had to remove all influences, environments, and people.

Does that sound harsh? I've been accused of being heartless, cruel, narcissistic, and naïve. Perhaps some of the criticism is deserved. I caused a great deal of pain to many people, especially family and friends. The guilt from those actions haunts me still.

My only rebuttal is that my decision never felt like a personal choice. Surrounded by despair and disappointment, an act this radical felt like the only option. It would hurt my family in the short term, I reasoned, but in the idealistic framework that consumed me, what we were doing would in time help my family and friends, working people like them, and the countless others I saw trodden upon and oppressed. Our overarching purpose was to reduce suffering and build a new world focused on the common good—a world without rulers, entirely democratic, based on merit, not inheritance, rooted in community, driven by compassion, truly entrepreneurial... The plan, we reassured each other, was for the greater good.

Giving in to significant doubts and accepting inaction would have been the mental and energetic death of me. With all other alternative paths relegated to certain futility, the nearly impossible was worth trying. We did not have any wise elders to deter us; at least, no wise elders we would want to listen to. Like extreme athletes, we were convinced we could achieve or defy the nearly impossible.

Today, more than forty-five years later, I still believe that the conspiracy hatched in my attic apartment was part of my destiny. I'd always known my otherness. When I decided to disappear, I was at a breaking point, and when the image of the dragon revealed itself to me, it felt like I finally understood my irresistible calling, a transcendent necessity that overrode any misgivings within myself. Focusing on personal or individual change was not enough to affect the systems that were destroying us all. We needed something radical, beyond the scope of history and egocentric ambition. And I was uniquely positioned to make that happen.

The disappearance felt like a calling from the universe and at least in part why I was born on planet Earth. In many ways, I still believe that. This wasn't just a political and economic revolution. It was an energetic or spiritual calling, a way to connect with the cosmos.

Yet, beneath those visions of purpose, a terror I prefer to some degree not to acknowledge motivated me. I knew I could successfully finish the fall semester of 1977, now that I had a plan to disappear. But if I didn't, in the winter semester of 1978, I knew for certain that I would cut all my classes, write no papers, take no tests. It would take a gun to my head to make me pass my classes so that I could graduate that year with a BA in German Studies I couldn't care less about. I would be immobilized by the terror of a life I could not tolerate. The shame and failure would crush me. The disappointment of teachers, friends, and family would be unendurable. I would become a street person who would end up succumbing to drug addiction. Insanity would soon take over, like the psychotics I worked with at the Northampton Mental State Hospital as a volunteer during my last semester at Deerfield Academy. When I asked the psychoanalytic psychiatrist who supervised me if I might harm them in any way because of my lack of training, he said that nothing I could do could harm them since they weren't really here. He then suggested I read some obtuse texts by Otto Fenichel.

On the other hand, even when events were filled with despair and there was no exit or expected to be so, I had always found a path out which opened doors I could never have anticipated would be available to me. Something to ponder: when is fear true, and when is it a melodrama that *seems* so very true?

* * *

We called ourselves the Nexalistic Revolutionary Front, or the NRF, and starting in October 1977, our plans came into existence with the ease of a prophecy. Over the course of a few weeks, Walter, Paul, and I worked out the organizational structure of the revolution. The way we saw it, the NRF would need two distinct branches. The Right Arm would represent the aboveground branches of business, politics, and religion. Meanwhile, what we called the Left Arm would create an underground presence that would work to empower the impoverished and downtrodden, uniting them into a sort of army to eventually overthrow the corrupt systems of power.

My role in the NRF was primarily to lead the development and expansion of the Left Arm and to function as a liaison between the

Left Arm and the aboveboard or outwardly legitimate actions of the Right Arm. My long-term mission was to start building a movement that would ultimately escalate tensions and demand the attention of those in key positions of power.

The operational details of our lofty goals remained unintentionally vague. What did we know about starting a revolution? Inciting dramatic change that could involve violence? Recruiting those willing to give up all they had? Call it confidence or the arrogance of youth, but there wasn't a lot of operational clarity, nor could there be given all the unknowns. We had to be intuitive and opportunistic with events and circumstances as they occurred. What were the procedures to become a global leader in government or the prophet of a world religion like Paul Atreides in *Dune* by Frank Herbert? That never came up.

There was no cookbook for revolutions, we told ourselves, and even if there were, those manuals were rooted in past failures and misperceptions. We would need to be fluid and contextual, trust one another, and make plans as events called us to adapt. That may have been a convenient rationalization with the purpose of keeping us on mission, but in an odd way, it was also an insightful one.

What we were planning was unheard of, unexplored, never done. No one could know what to expect. Expectations would only get in the way. Our only plan was to be open to perceive and then act on the opportunities the universe provided. At a transcendental or spiritual level, we wanted to harmonize with the unknown energies that permeated existence, the forces outside each bubble of reality, and discover if they could be interested in helping such insignificant and primitive creatures.

Our triumvirate focused on the importance of our cause, pumping ourselves up with bluster, which compensated for our insecurities and ignorance. Still, we rejected and abhorred the death trap of utopian aspirations. Our goals, like all aspirational goals, were to convince others of our cause, but first, we had to convince ourselves that we were on the right track.

We started writing top secret NRF documents that fall, outlining our core principles and beliefs. They described how Americans thoughtlessly live in the paradox of believing they are in a political democracy, with outcomes determined by elections, but in fact spend most of their lives in authoritarian institutions and corporations that are medieval, hierarchical, and anti-democratic. Our papers and discussions centered on democratizing all of society, even corporations. All leadership would be based on meritocracy in ways that would ensure accountability for even the most elite and powerful. We explored ideas for helping large groups of people to access the infinite possibilities within them and so reduce forms of societal control over them. Topics shifted rapidly; for instance, whether we should use the funds hitherto wasted on the military-industrial complex to finance more space travel. I wrote forcefully about replacing the money-based system of valuation with alternative systems that could not be manipulated by the charming sociopaths of wealth and power, taking inspiration from Ursula Le Guin's novel *The Dispossessed*, which portrays a society without money or ownership.

History-making is a fortuitous and capricious project, a nonlinear path of complex unknowns. A small event or decision can have colossal consequences. For the great, the wannabe great, and the not-great, history-making includes certain amounts of bumbling along the way. Even if the course of events was uplifting, tragic, or horrible in the end, moments of comedy and scathing sarcasm were already part of the NRF and thankfully would continue to counter the grandiosity.

* * *

At no time is a hierarchy of prerogatives and best-est and most-est gibberish to squirm its way into the machinery of the Party, i.e., philistine distinctions between business and personal life. This is an all-out holozoic monistic dedication and loudmouth frothing in the bleachers, not a holding-a-girl's-hand organization. Those who do not accept are to be reeducated.

**—From the Nexalistic Revolutionary Front (NRF)
Documents by Nathan T. Stanfield (NTS)
a.k.a. Steven Kubacki, 1978**

* * *

Walter and I had always agreed that the only safe place to discuss clandestine business was in a noisy bar or at a rock concert, like the one where I had first met him. The noise effectively insulated normal conversations from eavesdropping or listening bugs. In our favorite watering hole on a Friday night in Holland, you typically had to shout just to be heard by the person sitting across the booth. This was where we planned the greatest revolution the world might ever know.

"To our empire, and the chaos we will create," Walter raises his glass of beer.

Paul's eyes gleam. "Hope College will be famous. I can see it now: a statue of our faces melded in the heads and body of the dragon, standing in front of the student union. Who would have thought out of two Christian colleges three rogues like us would converge?" We laugh and clank our glasses.

I study both of my comrades. In time, I would be helping the Left Arm foment uprisings that could lead to revolution. Though not openly stated, I always understood that one of my primary duties was to make sure that these men, the Right, never lost sight of the mission. In my own uncertainty, I required a repeated reassurance that they would not waver on their individual ascents to success. Mostly, I accomplished this through memories of past conversations made more positive with internal pep talks to myself.

At one point that fall, Walter half-jokingly asks, "What happens if I become corrupted in the pursuit of Coin? What if when the time for revolution comes, I don't want to give up the good life?"

I tell him, half-jokingly, "I'd have to kill you. And who will suspect a ghost of murder?" And Walter, who knows corruption intimately, agrees.

It was a heady, exciting time of big dreams and daring action, though in hindsight, I can see that our experience together was bound more by rhetoric than strategy. Back then, I could not allow fissures to appear in the mission, though they were clearly there from the beginning and present within me.

This was a visceral quest as well as an existential one. We wanted to physically feel the revolution in our bones and muscles and so make it undeniably real and irreversible, like aging and death.

Then the revolution was not just a possibility in the mind, but a foregone necessity.

It would be "a leap of faith." A deed Kierkegaard would approve of, according to Paul, who admired existential Christianity.

* * *

To distract myself, perhaps, or to throw off suspicion, or simply because the opportunity arose, I traveled to Europe before Thanksgiving that year with a new friend, Frank McAdams.

Frank was an older guy, a few years retired and a widower, who lived near Hope. I don't remember how James and I met him—probably through one of James' many girlfriends. I was immediately drawn to his easygoing, fatherly nature. James and I would go to his house often for dinner, or he would drive us around the area in his giant Cadillac.

Frank lived alone and didn't have a family that I could see; his wife had died, and he never mentioned children or other relatives. He was financially comfortable after decades of hard work in a union job, and after a lifetime of saving and living frugally, he had dreams of a European tour. After he found out that I'd lived and traveled extensively in Europe, he would often ask me about my adventures there. He made me feel worldly and experienced.

One day, he told me about a fantasy he had held for a long time. "I want to eat dinner at the restaurant inside the Eiffel Tower, smoke a cigar, and look out over the city while a maître d' catches my ash on a silver platter." It was silly, perhaps, but for Frank, that cigar in the Eiffel Tower had become a symbol of his self-made success.

He asked me to travel with him to France, to be his guide. I would book all of the tickets and hotel rooms, drive the car, and take him to see the off-the-beaten-path sights, and he would pay for everything. It was a great deal, and I said yes immediately. We left two weeks later, right in the middle of the fall semester. We went to Venice and Berlin, where I visited an old German girlfriend, Eike. At first all went well with her, quite romantic, but shortly, at a café she accused me of being absent, as if I were somewhere else. I agreed. But my lack of denial or an excuse wasn't satisfying enough for the drama she wanted. She yelled, cursed, and left without a word. She was right to be angry, because I offered no explanation. Later, in Paris, Frank paid the Eiffel Tower maître d' 200 francs to hold a silver ashtray while he smoked his cigar.

I didn't tell anyone except James that I was going to France—not my friends or my professors or my family. My mother didn't find out I'd left the country until after I got back.

It was another of my disappearances in my short life for her to remember. One more unconscious slip of mine that would lead others, like my mother, to be suspicious later.

* * *

By the time the holidays rolled around, the three of us were setting our plan in motion. Walter started gathering money and supplies to fund my ventures. Walter recruited a friend from another college, Alex Linke, to help them collect supplies. Alex had a radical streak that made him an ideal co-conspirator and was far enough removed from me that no one would suspect him. He went to one of his acquaintances—a man none of the rest of us knew—to buy a getaway car, while Walter borrowed $3,000 from his father to help me get settled into my new life. Both of my friends stayed out of the limelight, and we made some efforts not to be seen exclusively together, in order to keep suspicion off them after my death. That wasn't so difficult, because Walter was at Calvin College in Grand Rapids most of the time and Paul was at the seminary. Hanging out a lot with James made it easier to create the appearance that there was nothing going on.

In that vein, I went out of my way to tell stories about my thrill-seeking adventures to anyone I met and bought a pair of cross-country skis. I also showed off my passport in public to reinforce my prior history of traveling to Europe whenever the mood struck me. Building a credible story that my passport was always on me would I thought diminish later questions of why it was missing.

For example, a year before, I'd skipped three weeks of classes to visit Eike, only to irk my professors by acing my final exams when I came back. Another time, when I left to visit Astrid and did not attend one class in Literature and Mysticism, I received As on my papers, an F for class participation, and was branded a C+ mystic for my final grade. I've been proud of that ever since: a people's mystic—slightly above average.

As 1977 turned into 1978, I spent long hours out on the frozen tundra of Lake Michigan, traveling light and ranging far, earning my reputation for taking risks. The time or two that I stayed out all night, I terrified James' girlfriend, an international student from the University of Kyiv who had grown up with stories of people who froze to death. That worked in our favor in the end, because she helped spread concern about my dangerous hobbies. Not that it was hard to convince anyone that I was inclined to dangerous pursuits and a few strange habits or ideas.

Curiously, at no point did I—or anyone else—bring Richard into the conspiracy or planning. He was a major part of the planned revolution—we expected him to become a great politician, after all—but we weren't sure when to get him involved. We thought at that point that the smaller the original core of conspirators was, the better—less chance of unintended mistakes. Besides, we weren't sure he would join before I disappeared. But afterwards, I felt certain he would, because then the disappearance would be real, and the force of its reality might make inclusion irresistible.

Richard hated the system like we did. He was a brilliant tactician, organizer, politician, and warrior and had the capacity to decisively act. He might admire our plan if he was included, but I was unsure of his commitment to a group of counterculture college students, who might potentially do what it takes to change the world, or might not. Trust in rhetoric has its limits.

In hindsight, I think I was worried that Richard would challenge the plan with realistic objections or alternatives, and without intending it, would undo our commitment. The NRF idealism, which bordered on the fantastical, could have been shattered by too much analysis. Realism has its place, but I thought then—and still believe today—that it also can be and is used to undermine and prevent action. The pathology of thinking—deferring action by obsessive and ruminative thinking—is why most people never dare to implement their ideas, ambitions, visions, and dreams, especially as they get older. There's always some reason not to act.

It would take a bit of theater to snap Richard out of the comfortable life he had in Atlanta, and so we agreed that Walter and Paul would sit down with him after my death. After all, what better theater is there than resurrection?

* * *

Waiting for the event was far harder than the event itself. I was giddy with anticipation and terrified about what my death would unleash. Not just the harm to my family: I tried not to think too much about that, though during Christmas break that year, I found myself gazing at each of them a little more intently than normal. Lying to my parents in those weeks was the hardest part of everything that happened, before and since. I had terrible nightmares for years afterward.

I was also obsessed with what would happen to me. The questions circling my mind became almost compulsive. What would it mean to disappear? How would I live without Steven's identity? His history? I would need to become a different person if I was to achieve the ends of the Left Arm. I might become a criminal. Could I become heartless and violent, or would I follow a path of nonviolence like Gandhi? Could I unify love and death in a transcendent ideal that did good, as I hoped, or was such good a delusion beneath which evil lurked?

These thoughts consumed me, and yet it all felt right—predestined—as if the wheel of my life was coming around to some inescapable outcome. Every trial and tribulation I'd been through—all of the pain, illness, sadness, and loneliness—had happened to prepare me for my own death, and perhaps with that death would come an unforeseeable gateway to the multiverse, where I might reconnect with my many selves.

In private, I tried to practice not responding to my given name, acting as if Steven Kubacki was a stranger, or already a ghost. I decided that my new name would be Nathan T. Stanfield.

* * *

And then, finally, the day arrived.

On the morning of February 19, 1978, I rose from my bed with unflinching intent. Though it was sunny, a storm had been forecast for Holland and its surrounding areas that evening, promising bitter cold and heavy snow. Most people took the weatherman's advice and hunkered down, which worked in my favor.

I left my apartment for the last time, carrying nothing but my cross-country skis and knapsack, and made my way to the edge of town, where the banks of the frozen lake jutted up like snowcapped burial mounds. I thought about the few people I saw along the way, and how they would soon become witnesses, crucial in the building of an official timeline of events. It's worth noting that my own self-importance got away from me here. In the end, not a single person came forward to remember seeing me that Sunday. Steven Kubacki passed through Holland for the final time like a ghost.

As I took to the lake, my thinking was simultaneously fragmented and laser focused. I was everywhere all at once, and nowhere to be found—already vanishing without a trace. I thought of myself only as Nathan T. Stanfield. It was Nathan who glanced over his shoulder to ensure that no one was in sight. Nathan who trembled despite the heavy jacket.

I felt supercharged in that moment, connected to all of humankind—to people alive and dead I did not know, though I was certainly no Buddha. I was so lit up I worried I might attract the attention of a powerful, otherworldly force. Imminent death is a powerful magic.

Eventually, my intuition told me that I'd found the right spot. I kicked off my skis and placed them beside the knapsack. As if sensing the finality of the moment, the blue sky disappeared, and the threatening snows finally came. Another stroke of fortune, because the storm would cover or make unrecognizable my foot tracks back to the shore. As the police later described, my tracks simply ended on the frozen lake far from the shore.

On the way back, Nathan had been careful to step into Steven's original tracks.

***

Hello Nate, it's Steven. Remember me? I know you can sense me, though you won't consciously hear these messages. They are entangled sets of photons, with which the photomorphic structures of your brain will decode. I've been invaded. It's not a bad thing. Our agenda and the agendas of the higher dimensional beings are in accord, but not by any intention of theirs. Ambassadors of good are directed your way — songs of light to harmonize with your songs of darkness. The Earth has its song, as do the stars, the individuals you meet, the clothes you wear, everything has its own song and together they form symphonies that you, Nate, will have a part in.

***

Steven stayed on the ice, dissociated. I could sense him traveling somewhere in the multiverse. I could not help him anymore but hoped that he or his friends would still help me.

I made my way to the park where Alex Linke had left the getaway car. And after all of the things that had gone right, that's where things started to go wrong. The car turned out to be a lemon, and its engine had frozen in the dropping temperatures and wouldn't start. It was a piece of junk. With this absurdity, I remember thinking long ago that Groucho Marx might be the son of God, and so in the mystery of the trinity, God was Groucho Marx. Like the wind that steadily increased, existence howled with a dark humor I could appreciate.

Certificate of Merit

To Alex Linke

For his accomplishments despite himself, his general indolence, and his chronic lack of imagination, we, the NRF, humbly known as the Organization, bestow upon him a raise in rank from Village Idiot to Party Dunce.

Well done, Alex!

I sat in the park for an hour, trying to decide what to do. The plan had been for me to drive away, undetected, in an anonymous vehicle, so that no one would witness me leaving town. But that was now impossible. I couldn't contact my co-conspirators, Alex, or anyone else I knew. Nathan, after all, didn't know anyone.

In the end, I had to take a risk. I pulled my parka hood over my face, hoped the snow would keep everyone indoors and away from their windows, and hiked back to town.

Luck stayed on my side. Even though I saw several people at various points on my trek back to Holland, no one connected the dots—not even the clerk at the Greyhound station where, using some of the money Walter had collected for me, I bought a ticket for the first bus leaving town.

It was going south to Mexico.

Chapter 6

THE JAGUAR

For navigating reality, we have lots of useful methods: science, logic, hermeneutics, analytic reasoning... It's navigating irrationality, the unknown, imaginary space, inconsistencies, fate, petty tyrants, karma, the seething, the transcendental, the trivial, quantum consciousness... What's terrifying and gratifying... That's what I need and am trying to make some sense of... I don't think I'm doing such a good job, but I'm trying my best... Tomorrow will be a better day... The Navajos have a ceremony Following a Path of Beauty... It's a long chant... Maybe I'll chant that in my dreams tonight... Though I probably won't remember... Navajos believe all our thoughts and nonthoughts continually chant the existence we know into being...

—From the Nexalistic Revolutionary Front (NRF) Documents by Nathan T. Stanfield (NTS) a.k.a. Steven Kubacki, 1978

I hunched low in the bus seat, my hood over my face, convinced at any moment that I would be recognized, that Steven Kubacki would be resurrected before he even had the chance to die.

By the time we crossed the Texas border, though, the heat was interminable, and I had to take my chances without a parka. By now, the Greyhound was full of laborers and lonely-looking cowboys. No one paid any attention to me.

Those long hours on the bus passed slowly and gave me plenty of time to consider what I'd done, what I was doing. Every time I fell asleep, animalistic dark forces attacked my mind. They reminded me of the hungry ghosts of Buddhism, spirits that were compulsively drawn to negative emotions and thoughts. I somehow knew that they'd found me because of the havoc I was wreaking upon my family and others. When Steven fell through the ice and I did not fall through, I entered an intense state of emotional and cognitive disassociation, which I believe created a temporal tunnel the hungry ghosts used to invade me.

I woke up several times screaming. The immense suffering I had unleashed felt like a bomb slamming into a small gathering of unsuspecting people. I could not calculate the collateral damage I had inflicted on my co-conspirators. I had invited familiar and new dark forces into my life, and they would be with me for many years to come.

* * *

At the border, the Mexican authorities waved me through without even bothering to stamp my passport—which, if they'd looked at it, would have identified me as Steven Kubacki.

Though this seems hard to believe from the perspective of the twenty-first century, in 1978, the NRF never even attempted to acquire false documents for me. I don't think we even talked about it. As much as I was emotionally and psychologically Nathan T. Stanfield for those fifteen months, whenever I crossed a border, I used the missing-and-presumed-dead Steven Kubacki's passport—*and no one ever noticed.* Perhaps this, more than anything else in my story, is a sign of how different life was in the pre-internet era. There were no global databases then, no ways to share or scan information that could be easily lost or incorrectly inputted, and really no way for a lonely Mexican border guard in Laredo to know that he was looking at a missing person from Michigan.

Once I'd safely crossed the border, I had to decide where to go next. I'd always known that I would go to Mexico first. It was the perfect place to hide while the news of my disappearance was still fresh. Mexico was easy to access, inexpensive, and most importantly, the last place anyone would think to look for me. My travels up to that point in my life had always taken me over the ocean to Europe. Everyone knew I spoke German fluently, but not a word of Spanish.

This later turned out to be a good choice. In the investigations after my death, official inquiries were made at airports, looking for anyone with my description flying to Germany. Many people who doubted my death assumed I was in Europe. No one ever thought to check the Greyhound schedules or tickets.

But now here I was, standing in front of the giant map on the bus station wall. Mexico was a big country. Where should I go?

I settled on Monterrey, for no reason other than it was a big city, but not as big as Mexico City. It was also close to Laredo, and there was a bus leaving the terminal soon.

A few hours later, I was walking through the muddy streets of Monterrey, realizing that none of my previous travels had prepared me for Mexico. While I'd always been painfully aware that I wasn't part of the wealthy class, I'd never been exposed to real poverty, either. Here in Monterrey, I witnessed levels of deprivation unlike anything I'd seen. Urine and excrement streamed down the middle of the steep, hilly street, and the air was full of smoke from both propane stoves and the surrounding factories.

But I noticed something else as I walked aimlessly through the barrios and slums of Monterrey. Even here, people sat in their shacks and listened endlessly to the radio. Some even had televisions. And then I noticed the men with wheelbarrows loaded with cases of Coca-Cola, struggling up and down the hill. I saw that the residents, obviously destitute, would emerge and flock at their passing, the way American children run toward an ice cream truck. They were caffeinated and hooked.

The Culture Industry had infiltrated even here.

I still remember my feeling of outrage and how it drowned out my fear and guilt. Why did people put up with this? They were literally living in their own shit while drinking the branded product of their oppressor. No wonder there were no revolutions happening here. Everyone had already been bought out.

Eventually, I found a dingy hotel in the Barrio Antiguo, paid cash for two weeks in advance, and fell face first onto a bed that was only relatively clean. Exhausted and emotionally drained, I sobbed before slipping once more into a troubled sleep. I dreamed about my mother, wailing into television news cameras and grieving the death of her son.

The next day, I walked the city streets in a kind of limbo. I checked the newspapers for word of my disappearance, though I knew it was too soon for the story to have spread so far. Back in my room, I wrote poetry that doubled as manifestos for the NRF. I was lonely and desperate to reinforce my decision and cast away any wavering.

After a few days of hiding, it was time to get to work. I'd heard that someone who lived in my hotel had been beaten badly by a street gang, and that sent my anxiety spiking again. Martial arts training, I realized, would serve two purposes to get the Left Arm off the ground. I couldn't recruit and train a cadre of liberators if I didn't know how to fight. But also, I might need it to keep me safe personally.

I asked a few people on the street to recommend a local dojo and then followed their directions to a small concrete building, about the size of an American two-car garage. The instructors, or Sempai, were a mix of Mexican and Chinese martial artists, and they welcomed me. The younger athletes and instructors fortunately spoke enough English, though they told me that were no other Americans studying at the dojo at the moment. I took that as another good sign, since I didn't want to attract the attention of anyone watching American media. For just $5 a week, I signed up to access the gym any time I wanted and got as much instruction as I could handle.

Too much instruction, I started to realize.

* * *

I brushed aside the dojo masters' questions about what an American like me was doing in the slums of Monterrey. I introduced myself as Nathan Stanfield from Ohio and said I'd been drawn here because I needed to get away, wanted a different life from what I'd known before. I hinted at personal tragedy and heartbreak. The Sempai thought I was odd, I could tell, but I was used to that. Ultimately, they accepted me. They started inviting me over to their houses for dinner almost every night but never seemed bothered when I declined. I wasn't ready to get close to anyone.

I dove into my training, spending all day, every day at the gym. I'd never had formal training in martial arts or any type of fighting, and I just ate it up. I recall in the third grade at recess that I would sometimes act like a ninja with a group of friends, who I invited to attack me en masse and not hold back. Somehow, I was able to dodge and throw one into another onto the grassy ground and avoid being captured. I was an athlete at Deerfield in football, track, and gymnastics, where I lettered as a freshman and became a tri-captain in my senior year.

After just two weeks in the dojo, I was getting the hang of karate. I loved to spar. At the end of the day, my body was so tired that it was all I could do to stumble back to my hotel room, where the hungry ghosts were always ready to embrace me. I slept terribly.

As the days went by, I started to notice some odd things about the dojo.

The instructors seemed to spend all of their time together, for one thing, even outside the gym. And I started to notice that they all had tattoos of snakes, either winding around their upper arms or spreading across their chests near their hearts.

Meanwhile, there was a steady flow of people coming into the building who clearly weren't there to work out. Instead, they disappeared into the office in the back. Some other kind of business was happening back there, I decided. Was it the mundane crime of selling drugs, or was it something else, something that touched other realms and possibilities?

Bit by bit, the dojo and its mysterious back room started to carry a dark vibe. I wondered if the instructors were all *brujos*, or practitioners of the local occult religion known as *brujería*, a mix of spirituality and dark magic that is similar to Haitian voodoo. *Brujos* are sorcerers, able to cast spells and call on spirits, and what was happening in the back room did not feel like healing to me. I could tell that there were negotiations, and I saw the head guy—his nickname was Cuchillo—giving a handful of feathers to someone.

My suspicions appeared to be confirmed when Cuchillo pulled me aside and told me that they had been expecting me when I arrived the first time. I thought at first that it was a translation error, because Cuchillo couldn't have known I was coming when I didn't even know myself. Still, I was understandably paranoid. Had he heard about my disappearance somehow? Did he know who I really was?

When I pressed him to say more, the Sempai told me that one of the teachers had seen a jaguar in a dream a few days before I showed up. Cuchillo said they had been waiting for a jaguar to come ever since, and now he was sure it was me.

I took a breath, relieved that he knew nothing about Steven Kubacki, but still concerned that this *brujo* saw something more in me than I'd expected him to perceive. He could see the energy surging through me, maybe the hungry ghosts chasing me. I was convinced that he could sense both the idealism and rage still coursing through me. He knew that part of me wanted to save the world, but another part still wanted to annihilate it.

And that was a tempting source of power for someone like Cuchillo.

That night, the dark forces came after me with menacing but seductive force.

I am being invaded, filled with things not me, overpowered with energy I should not crave. Something or someone is inside me, trying to take over, to convince me that my will can be greater united with its will. But I resist and wake up shaken with the sense of threat. Though the darkness guesses that I want power, it does not realize I fear control by anyone or anything more.

I cannot tolerate being controlled for long. Many bosses, and many more women, have tried. While I accommodate them to a point, eventually I resist and rebel, sometimes in a conflagration of drama, sometimes withdrawing, and sometimes enclosing myself behind a protective mask that tells them what they want to hear so I can eventually escape.

Now, I was not just fighting off nightmares about my grieving mother but also internalizing new combat skills to mentally fight off forces that wanted to enhance me by occupying me.

The next day in Monterrey, a few of the instructors that I had now come to know as *brujos* wanted to talk to me while I was taking a break. They struck up a friendly conversation, but I was weary and wary, on guard from the previous night's invasion. I instinctively knew that they had been behind it. These were my dream invaders in corporeal form.

Casually, one of the instructors pointed to his snake tattoo and asked if I would like to have one like it. Before I could answer, it seemed as if the artwork detached itself from the *brujo*'s skin and moved around, turning its head to look at me appraisingly.

Was this an initiation? An invitation to a cult? Had the previous night's attack been designed to wear down my defenses with the seduction of power, so that I would be more likely to join whatever they were doing?

I brushed off their conversation and left the dojo earlier than usual that day. There were some things about the *brujo*'s offer that were tempting. I missed having a cohort of allies nearby, and I was intrigued by the classic magic they were doing in the back rooms. People join groups like this for a reason, and I was not immune. I wanted to feel connected. I wanted to belong, just like anyone else. I wanted the power of this group and the knowledge of how to heal myself and others. It would have been easy to become absorbed.

But the price, I already knew, was too high. To join them, I would have to give up major parts of my being to serve the shamanic powers they had captured. Or did I have it all wrong: was it *brujos* who were captured by those powers from other dimensions and in their egoism couldn't see it? Either way, I would have to give up the NRF—sacrifice my integrity, my destiny, my commitment to bringing about radical change.

What was happening in Monterrey felt like genuine shamanism on one hand, but I also sensed the local shenanigans of petty people. Local spiritual politics were involved, and I wasn't interested in that. My calling was to change the entire planet.

If they made their offer official in person, I knew there would be consequences if I refused. The menace was real, mentally if not physically. But how to hold them off without giving away my own secrets?

That night, I set a trap in my lucid dreams for the invading forces. When they came, I confronted them with light and demanded that they reveal themselves, as well as their intent.

I wasn't prepared for what I learned, though. It was definitely the *brujos*, and I discovered they'd been coming to my dreams every night since I first went to the dojo, stealing energy from my parallel lives—those other realities that had been so close to my consciousness recently.

Most people imagine our existence like floating down a river, moving from one life to the next. But in actuality, time is not linear. Everything is happening simultaneously across the multiverse—meaning there is no river, but instead an endless ocean of alternative histories we jump to and from, generally without awareness.

We don't have "past lives," in other words, despite what pop culture tells us about "past life regression." Instead, we're living all of our lives simultaneously, and "past lives" are really the alternative lives we're recalling from another reality. The *brujos* sought to draw power from me because they could see these connections and the power that came through them.

When they realized that I could see them, the *brujos* retreated. And another vision emerged.

There's a full moon tonight, and I am surrounded by dense green undergrowth. Water is flowing beneath my feet. Large green eyes appear far in the distance. They are looking for me. Quietly they move and cross a nearby stream. I hide behind giant ferns. I try not to make a sound.

Suddenly it's on top of me. I'm thrilled but scared. It licks my face with a scratchy wet tongue. A gaping mouth opens. Into it I fall. Its massive teeth shred my flesh and bones, but I feel no pain.

My body seems to dissolve. I disperse. I'm in the trees, the streams, the sky, the night, the stars. I feel so free...

There's a shift in the scenery. Around me I hear raindrops, insects, frogs. I feel the ferns glide against my body. I can see everything in the dark. I am running fast. I see a deer and leap upon it. I slash its throat and eviscerate its stomach with my paws.

I wake up. I'm not in the jungle.

But I am a jaguar.

And the Jaguar has come for me.

I recognized the Jaguar from the stories and totems of the ancient cultures I had studied. I'd read works by the anthropologist Carlos Castañeda and was drawn especially to his books *Journey to Ixtlan* and *The Teachings of Don Juan*. They'd opened my perspective to how power could be acquired by giving up a part of the self, the potential and consequences of wheeling and dealing with the spirit world—a kind of spiritual capitalism, where serious sorcery could lead to death and worse, but most importantly for now, to a visitation from Jaguar.

I'd never seen a Jaguar before personally, but I recognized him right away as Jaguar from the stars, what others might call a spirit. He appeared because I needed protection, which I needed at that moment in Monterrey more than ever.

Jaguar said I had to move on, that the dojo was no longer a safe place for me, that my guilt and my nightmares had made me weak and vulnerable. It was time to travel east, the Jaguar said, to recover the alternative life energy that the *brujos* had drained from me. I would need to recover it if I ever wanted to be successful. This is what I gleaned, though verbally nothing was said.

The visit made it clear that it was time to pursue my mission with more focus and intention—that my time in Mexico was not helping me understand what needed to be done.

The next morning, I left Monterrey. I didn't tell anyone I was going, and I never went back to that dojo. I simply packed my bag and went to the bus station to go east, as Jaguar had said.

My first stop was Mexico City to get a travel visa. My ultimate destination, though, was as far east as I could imagine: Japan.

* * *

I am walking through shades of light. They are all light. Some are like the light we experience on Earth. But in another dimension, in this continuum of energy, there are many kinds of light. Some construct the appearance of walls, floors, and ceilings, though you can see through them to other forms of light and beyond that to colored lights of myriad hues. I wonder where those colors lead.

Don't get me wrong. The entire continuum of light—an energy shell, as I have labeled it—is pervasive throughout, so there is only light, no absence of light. Because of this, there are no two-dimensional surfaces. In my perceptions, limited as they are to human perception, they seem to be three-dimensional, but intuitively I know they encompass more, including time.

In the energy shell, the light is alive in the multidimensional surfaces, in everything. Patterns of light coalesce together to form what we think of as bodies. I perceive myself as a human body of light. I am the Steven of Light.

There are other bodies of light, but their shapes are constantly changing. My shape is probably also changing, but I don't see it.

Some of these bodies of light I call the Others. I could project onto them the usual forms people see—angels, devils, aliens with big heads and eyes and long necks, emitting the emotions of love or fear—that is, anything people have read about or seen at the movies or on TV. But I resist. I'm a Nexalist, not a believer or a paranoid. Still, one appears like a jaguar.

Chapter 7
THE DARK MONK

My friends, don't ever be taken off guard. The dialectics of disaster are upon us. Though the neon signs of the coming disaster glare, screaming with viscid colors to turn our heads and look at them, we instead deny their imminence and fixate on the illusion that we are in control of the situation. Rather than avert, avoid or stave them off, we should accept them and use them to our advantage. Such an attitude requisites a 'no-step' awareness, wherein ideas and plans retain their status of tools rather than our Masters; kinda like in Cinderella at the coming of a midnight disaster, they also retain their status as necessary self-deceptions, to be discarded at the stroke of twelve. Then we will have embraced the disasters before they embrace us, enabling us to redirect them to open new avenues of transformation rather than them just crushing us. In short, when you make the inevitability of disaster your best friend, that friend will guide you to incredible places and results you can never have imagined.

—From the Nexalistic Revolutionary Front (NRF)
Documents by Nathan T. Stanfield (NTS)
a.k.a. Steven Kubacki, 1978

I arrived in Mexico City driven by an intense urgency to get as far away from the *brujos* and their dark magic as I could, as quickly as I could. I wasn't sure whether the trap I'd set for them in my dream would be enough to break the tie they had on me. Was I confusing their shady dealings to extract profits for healing with my perceptions of their sorcery attacking me, thereby only creating illusions of my own that had no basis?

When I reached the capital, I gathered myself fully into the present moment and carried that energy straight to the Japanese consulate. To travel east, as Jaguar required, I needed a visa, and the only way to do that was to show my student identification.

I held my breath as the man in the suit took the card. It had been just a few weeks since my disappearance, and I had no idea how much of a stir my absence had created. Were there people searching for me still? Had my picture, my name, flashed onto televisions across the country? Beyond the borders? Could this serious-looking Japanese bureaucrat possibly know the significance of this little card identifying Steven Kubacki from Hope College?

I willed myself to be Nathan, to act as if I never had parents or friends. I drew upon the words of Don Juan in Castañeda's *Journey to Ixtlan*, who said that the freedom to achieve the impossible requires erasing all personal history. Only by doing so can we be liberated from all expectations and definitions of the self, including the constraints of everyday reality.

The bureaucrat's face never changed as he stamped his approval on my application for a student visa.

I went directly to the airport, where I saw that there were two flights to Japan leaving that day—one departing for Tokyo, the other for Osaka. For a moment, I was filled with uncharacteristic hesitation. Jaguar had only said to go *east*. Where would the Left Arm best be served?

As if in reply to my uncertainty, a group of stewardesses in Japan Air Line uniforms strolled past. One caught my eye, and without thinking, I picked up my duffle bag and followed her long, graceful legs to her gate—the flight to Osaka. It was a sign from the universe, and I went straight to the counter and asked to buy a seat on that flight. The beautiful stewardess even came over to help me, translating my desire in more ways than one. I ignore signs from the universe at my peril, so I try not to miss them; and anyway, they are almost always right.

Things moved quickly between us on that nearly twenty-four-hour flight. She came by several times to chat, despite the grumbles of passengers trying to sleep. Her name was Izumi. I introduced myself as Nathan. By hour five, I was writing poetry for her on scraps of paper, which I folded into clumsy origami birds. At hour seven, she pulled me into the back of the plane and kissed me behind the curtain.

In that secluded corner of the plane, surrounded by nothing but open sky and sleeping humans, I told her I was on my way to Japan to save the world. She laughed. Grinning, I told her I didn't have a place to stay for the night and that I needed help finding a monastery. She looked at me with astonishment and left. She returned briefly and told me to meet her after getting through customs, where she would be waiting to help me.

When I cleared customs, I saw her, and she beckoned me to follow her. We got into a cab and went to her apartment. I was surprised as I thought she was going to let me off at a hotel. She must have felt sorry for me. However, after tea and miso soup, we experienced the slow and irresistible game of inhibiting and disinhibiting desire. A few years older than me and obviously more experienced, Izumi was an artist of touch, and she taught me subtle arts that afternoon. Great sex always involves great heart, but this was the first time I experienced a connection as not just physical, but a union of consciousness and awareness that transcended physicality. After, I fell into a deep and dreamless sleep, free from nightmares or spiritual attacks.

The next day, Izumi asked about my plan to save the world, and I impulsively made a choice that, on its surface, was wildly dangerous and potentially stupid.

I told her everything.

I told her about the NRF and our goal to overthrow corrupt systems and create a new political and economic order. The three-headed dragon. Walter and Paul and Richard. Disappearing on the ice, and my mission to create the Left Arm of the revolution in order to sow seeds of chaos and redemption. The words, bottled up for weeks in Nathan's lonely existence, poured out of me.

Izumi listened carefully, her eyes never leaving my face, her expression giving away nothing. Finally, when I finished, she shook her head.

"You cannot save the world," she told me, "Because you don't have enough compassion to destroy it first."

I must have looked confused, because she continued. Compassion was power expressed indirectly and subtly, but I was acting with the drama and directness of Americans. That would only lead to resistance from others. A path that was more harmonious with the flow of change would cultivate compliance in others.

Her words flowed over me, and I understood why Jaguar had brought me here. Subtlety and indirectness, I acknowledged, had never been strengths of mine. I could *empathize* with the downtrodden of the world and feel their collective pain and frustration. But then I *overidentified* with those emotions, becoming reactive and dramatic, rather than letting them flow through me and guide me so I could lead them. I couldn't step far enough away from my own experience and feelings to influence the bigger picture. I had to face it. I was not a very good leader yet.

That day with Izumi, I forced myself to acknowledge that to be the Left Arm meant I would have to hurt people to help people. Could I be that compassionate, not to any person, but to the cause? Could I hurt others without hating myself afterwards?

I had to. For the NRF to succeed as I had designed it, my responsibility to humanity was to be ruthless for the greater good.

I would need to dramatically change my personality to pave the way for upheaval and perhaps bloodshed.

I noticed a small shrine in the corner of Izumi's kitchen, and the image of the yogi and poet Milarepa came to my mind—a despised and brutal murderer in his early years, who had turned to Buddhism and become a great spiritual teacher and monk in later life. If Milarepa could learn to live with his misdeeds through Buddhist practices, I decided, I could too.

I asked Izumi if there were any places in Osaka that combined Buddhist principles with martial arts training—the kind of warrior monastery that trained fighting monks of centuries past.

Izumi, of course, knew of just such a place, a type of residential Buddhist dojo that was known for taking on foreign students. We spent one last memorable night together, entwined into a visceral mandala of sand that the sunlight scattered in the early morning, and then she led me to the gate of a modern-looking compound deeply shadowed by the tall apartment blocks all around it. We said goodbye with a kiss.

* * *

i was thinking of revising the moon
to fit in with my plans
of world domination
but i realized that our relationship
could not overcome
the emptiness
that lay between

—From the Nexalistic Revolutionary Front (NRF)
Documents by Nathan T. Stanfield (NTS)
a.k.a. Steven Kubacki, 1978

* * *

It was not what I expected a Zen dojo to look like. The concrete and halogen streetlights clashed with the images I'd had of pagoda roofs and ancient symbolism, but I trusted the powers that had brought me this far, so I rang the bell and waited beside a dingy metal door. Eventually, a young and serious monk in a long white robe led me into an unadorned room. I knelt, ready for Nathan's next step of discovery.

The Sensei arrived after what seemed like a long wait. He sat across from me speaking in rapid-fire Japanese that I couldn't understand. He was a stern-faced older man with a shaved head and cloudy eyes. He looked disgusted with me.

Still, a younger monk standing behind him wrote a number—the cost of my tuition, I assumed. After doing a little mental currency conversion, I could hardly suppress my reaction. Were they testing me, or was the cost of enlightenment really ten times as much in Osaka as it had been in Monterrey? The flight to Japan had already taken a significant chunk of my NRF funds.

I took the pen and wrote a number of my own that was half of what they'd quoted.

The cloudy-eyed man in charge—the Sōke—considered the paper and then me. Eventually, he rose and gestured for me to follow him.

I was admitted. Accepted. Worthy.

I was pleased to discover that the ugly concrete building was not the primary campus for this monastic dojo. My new monk instructors took me directly to the train station. About an hour outside the city, we arrived at a much more traditional-looking compound in the wooded mountains. Walls were made of rice paper, and the paths were dotted with shrines and plants. This, they gestured, was where I would live and train.

I slept on the floor of an empty training room, with only a thin mat between me and the cold ground. The next morning, a young monk came and led me to the center courtyard. The Sōke was there, and as soon as he saw me, he rang a bell. Dozens of young men, some in robes but most wearing modern clothes, poured out of the doors and lined up in rows, perfectly still—at attention. I wondered if I was the only American there.

Someone brought out a plank of wood that was about an inch thick—like the kind I'd seen martial artists in Monterrey breaking with their bare hands. It was a trick I'd never learned.

The Sōke called me to stand in front of the assembled students. He held the board in both hands and shouted something at me. I didn't move. Another Sensei made a punching motion, striking the empty air before him encouragingly. I looked back to the Sōke and he nodded.

The courtyard was silent.

In the moment, Nathan Stanfield was deadly serious. He had a mission—to learn the fighting skills and Zen practices that would save the world. He could already see how this disciplined, rural, anonymous space could be a valuable place to stay for a while.

The part of me that was Steven, on the other hand, was overcome with how ridiculous I must look, standing there with all eyes on me. The rebellious trickster in me emerged, and I couldn't resist the urge to take the piss out of everyone there.

Positioning myself before the cloudy-eyed Sōke, I made a little bow. He returned the gesture, then held the board at arm's length again. I let loose a battle cry that surprised everyone, rushed forward, and rammed my head against the board. A collective gasp filled the courtyard.

The board remained intact, and I could feel blood on my forehead.

The Sōke looked at me for a long time. His disapproval was obvious, but eventually he nodded. I could stay.

My mat was moved to a dormitory room, where I slept on the floor with six other trainees, none of whom spoke English. We rose at 4:00 a.m. and ran through the Japanese mountains for two hours, then gathered in the courtyard for martial arts training. New students like me were drilled in the basics of hand-to-hand combat, while not far away, I could see more advanced students learning to wield classic Japanese weapons. I looked forward to the day when someone would give me a sword.

After we disciplined our bodies, we gathered for a meager meal and then settled in front of a shrine for long hours of meditation to discipline our minds.

At first, it seemed idyllic—this discipline of the body and mind was exactly what I needed to harden myself for my Left Arm duties, and the countryside itself was wooded and beautiful, full of ancient history, statues, arches, and energies. But within a couple of weeks, I began to struggle with monastic life.

My first sin was that I couldn't sit cross-legged for any real length of time, and lotus position—which the Sōke demanded during meditation—was physically impossible. He viewed my inflexibility as a sign of unworthiness. He cut my already limited food rations and hovered near me during my training, ready to strike me with a wooden rod any time I fell out of line.

I smarted at his rebukes. What had seemed like spiritual training at first started to feel like nothing but an attempt to manipulate me. It was textbook "high control"—deprive a group of proper food, sleep, and freedom, and you break them down. Their egos shrink until they lose any sense of self-importance and identity. There are benefits to this, of course, especially in military or spiritual settings—shrinking the ego helps a person to let go of attachments in the material world. But it can turn dark too. Once you break a person's ego, there's nothing stopping you from rebuilding them into whatever you want them to be—a weapon, a devotee, a puppet.

There were days when the Sōke would send us back into Osaka, dressed in our robes. We'd kneel or sit in a park somewhere, meditating with little baskets in front of us. People would walk by and put money in the baskets. Sometimes, we'd sell trinkets. We had to take the money back to the school and give it to the Sōke.

I could see it was a scam, because we were already paying for our training, and it was doubly insulting because Buddhism taught us to not seek wealth or prioritize material things. But the other trainees didn't see it that way. If the Sōke said something, it must be true.

My Buddhist dojo was starting to feel more like a cult.

As my resentfulness deepened, I reverted to a familiar attitude of rebellion. I would wake up before anyone else and ring the courtyard bell in the predawn dark to disorient everyone else. I brought a chair to the afternoon meditation and refused to sit on the ground. I gave away my daily food rations to the weakest of my fellow students. As punishment, the Sōke nearly doubled the number of drills and running one day, then made me spend the night standing on a large rock in the courtyard. If my mind drifted in its exhaustion, I would fall. I fell a lot. The whole scene reminded me of when I was a young teenager and would stand on a fence pole near my house for long minutes that felt like hours.

In the Zen rock garden, under the turning dome of heaven, I fought off my hunger and my exhaustion, and I tried to find meaning in the immensity of it all.

Had I made a mistake? What was I even doing there? I thought that a Zen dojo would be a place of selflessness and physical discipline, but I was caught up in the same control games that I'd seen in Mexico. Was there anything, really, that I could learn from a group of people so caught up in their petty struggles that they couldn't see the world beyond their dojo walls? Was this really the reality that I wanted to change?

* * *

It is time that Zen liberate itself from the womb of the monastery. In the old days monasteries were tough, begging was the trade. Now they are sanctuaries for the disenfranchised, the insecure, and those desperate to believe without question and surrender their souls; a locality wherein escapism and the quiet life can be led and all responsibility to the suffering of humankind abandoned with false but feel-good ineffectual intentions.

The heart of Zen is ruthless compassion. The Zen monk goes where it is the toughest. In the old days that used to be in mountains, caves, and even the harshness of the monastery. But for today's compromised monks, there are no more mountains of transcendence and rebirth. They are but places to market their goods. Now there are only tourists, backpackers, and climbers with ice axes in the tree-bare, high elevations, all of whom are driven to the energy and connectedness of nature. But no Zen monks.

Consequently, I envision the rebirth of the Zen spirit in the framework of the Nexalist, the release of Zen knowing to the enlightenment of all sentient beings, and if necessary, in the body of the death commando. A conclave of zealous, wild-eyed, death-disinterested monks would be a masterful achievement toward changing the world.

—From the Nexalistic Revolutionary Front (NRF)
Documents by Nathan T. Stanfield (NTS)
a.k.a. Steven Kubacki, 1978

* * *

Had I misunderstood the Jaguar when he said that I would find what the *brujos* had taken—the parallel lives that would make me into the compassionate killer that Izumi had described? Was that even possible here, under the Sōke's "enlightened" determination to destroy my attachments so I could attain Zen no-self and sell trinkets?

Late in the evening, while I balanced on a large rock in the Zen courtyard, an answer came. I had fallen several times, scattering the sand that was carefully raked twice a day, leaving disharmonious footprints and fissures instead. That stress added to the chronic stress I was already experiencing. As a result, a dormant strand of what I would later call "transdimensional DNA" was activated. "Transdimensional DNA" I hypothesized to be a kind of "genetic code" that connects us to our other alternative histories and timelines in the multiverse.

With this activation, a being appeared in my mind. He wasn't a foreign or alien energy. He was what I was seeking, familiar, with a resemblance to the darkness that had followed me through childhood. I knew this being, for he was some version of me from a higher dimensional universe.

He was dressed like a monk, like the Sōke, but there was something unsettling about him—something dark and renegade. Detached. Strong. Ruthless. I realized this parallel version of me intimately knew Izumi's lesson about the difference between empathy and compassion. Moreover, I could feel how he'd put that knowledge to use. The Dark Monk, as I would call him, was not empathetic, but coldly compassionate. He could—and had—done terrible things for what he believed was the greater good, actions far darker than me disappearing on the ice and allowing loved ones to think I was dead. He drew power that came from taking life.

His impeccable acts of ruthlessness made the Dark Monk formidable, but as we drew together like ghosts in the moonlight, I smelled in that ruthlessness the stench of corruption that could not be hidden in the shadows of his hooded dark robe. It reminded me of the putrid fragrances in funeral homes.

I have come to understand that just like the goateed man wielding levers who I'd met in my earlier vision on Mt. Washington, the Dark Monk version of me existed in other places. He was not only a complex confluence of this timeline and others, this dimension and others, but also functioned as a living archetype that affected humanity.

In that moment, standing on that Zen rock, all I could see was why Jaguar had deemed it so important to recover this other me. The Dark Monk was the vision of what I needed to become if the Left Arm was to succeed.

I became both delirious with power and terrified of that power.

There was nothing left for me to discover at the school. As the Jaguar had commanded me to do, I had found my stolen parallel selves in the Dark Monk.

That revelation came just in time. The very next morning, a fellow student—half-Korean with some basic English—whispered that the Sōke had been asking other students about me: where I'd come from in America, and why I was there. He had even started rumors about a lapsed visa or a fake identity and had probably searched my belongings while I was on the rock the night before.

There was plenty of time left on my student visa, but the identity question was dangerous. I was glad I kept my passport with me at all times and that the Sōke couldn't read English, making my notebooks useless to him. But he was clever and suspicious. The jig was up.

I had only been in Japan for a few weeks, but I decided that the risk of being overseas was too great. It had been naïve to think that

I could fulfill a secret mission and stay under the radar in a country where I didn't speak a word of the language.

The very next morning, I crept out of the rural training grounds before sunrise, and was back in Osaka, knocking on Izumi's apartment door, by noon. It was sheer luck that she was home.

Using the very last of the NRF dollars, I bought the cheapest one-way ticket to the United States that I could afford. But not all was lost. As I boarded my flight for Honolulu, Hawaii, in April, I felt the presence of the Dark Monk inside me.

* * *

Having passed through US customs untainted and safe, I commence a program in Honolulu of skin conditioning (tanning — fuck does this sunburn hurt like hell), running, and swimming. At this moment I am living on the beach, sleeping beneath the stars with crabs at my head. Still, what is the purpose to rebirth when the person in question is unable to take advantage of his remarkable circumstances? What is his freedom, when he regulates it to fanciful plans, having severed the means to substantiation? When will the ice that interlocks reason melt, and their fluids gasify into random molecules of incoherency and aimlessness, drifting and waiting for the coming assemblage of their purposes, and with that, concerted action? A dog could perform better than this lump of flesh. The limbic intrusion of loss and melancholic failure once debilitating on the beach has turned into indifference. That indifference, however, is priceless, because in its container turn uncut gems of no current market value. Those gems are waiting to be mined and unleashed. Meanwhile the *future — the unknowable unknown — laughs at our contrivance of a planned continuance.*

—From the Nexalistic Revolutionary Front (NRF)
Documents by Nathan T. Stanfield (NTS)
a.k.a. Steven Kubacki, 1978

* * *

I arrived in Hawaii with little money, no plan, and a deep sense of failure.

First, I'd fled Mexico, and then Japan. My grand mission was going nowhere. My training had barely started. Yes, my time at the warrior monastery had shrunk my ego enough for the Dark Monk to emerge, but it had also left me fragile. I was still torn between trying to save the world and trying to destroy the world, just as I was trying to save and destroy myself.

I had been broken down, but that was only half the work. Now the real challenge had to begin—how to fill the negative space. The Sōke had wanted to fill the space with subservience and dedication to their ways, but I'd left before he could do that.

Now, I was in a vacuum.

I still felt the sense of purpose and destiny that had guided me since Lake Michigan, but now it felt ancient, like it was something guiding me from long ago. Nathan had lost his way. The universe was no longer guiding me in the right direction.

I went from the airport to the beach and lived like a bum, sleeping outside every night with the bugs and crabs. During the day, I wrote manically.

I wrote poetry to try and romanticize things, but that didn't really help. Instead, I threw myself into rethinking the NRF. As naïve as this sounds, until that point, I'd been trusting the forces inside me to show me the next move, and I hadn't looked any further than that. Actions and thinking dominated by serendipity, synchronicity, idealism, and intuition had filled us all in the last months of 1977, and that mode was deeply ingrained in my mind. We magically thought we could change the world simply with the force of our collective wills. But now, with failure everywhere, I started to wonder if I needed a more concrete and circumspect plan.

I shifted from poetry to detailed timelines and structured lists. I still had no idea what I was doing—what did I know about staging a revolution? But getting an order of operations on paper felt like progress.

Many a night, the Dark Monk came to me in my dreams, admonishing me for my weakness—for *our* weakness. He accused me of hiding in fear and depression rather than embracing the power he offered. He said that without me—without us—the NRF would die.

He continued to terrify me, but he also drove me.

And furthermore, I emphatically deny and denounce such conceptual mismanagement as Guru and Enlightenment, Master and Monk, Doctrine and Path as hackneyed agents of oppression, legitimizing servility and creative retardation. Marxism, bowdlerized or authentic, are co-features to Water-on-the-Brain and Emphysema of the Cognitive Faculties.

—From the Nexalistic Revolutionary Front (NRF)
Documents by Nathan T. Stanfield (NTS)
a.k.a. Steven Kubacki, 1978

* * *

You cannot liberate yourself unless you likewise liberate your environment in the process. God is not dead, but he can no longer mend and clean your diapers. Lifetime professional scientists, monks, bureaucrats, and cowards of the world accept your social inheritance and irritations with the people. Come out swinging with your words, fists, and money. You are not alone. My gun is right beside you . . .

—From the Nexalistic Revolutionary Front (NRF)
Documents by Nathan T. Stanfield (NTS)
a.k.a. Steven Kubacki , 1978

* * *

This continued for weeks. I filled pages but accomplished little else. I don't know what would have happened to me—to Nathan—next, if the universe hadn't sent me a sign.

Early one morning, I took a swim on the deserted beach where I'd slept the night before. Everything seemed fine at first. In fact, it seemed like swimming was easier than it had ever been. I was gliding incredibly fast through the water. I was full of energy, moving with a coordination I'd never felt.

But then, as I got farther from shore, I stopped moving my arms and legs for a second, and realized I was still moving out toward the open water. I was caught in a riptide. No one else was in the water.

I turned and tried to power my way back toward the beach, but the current was too strong. Fighting panic, I tried to remember anything I'd ever heard about open water swimming. *You can't fight the current,* a voice in my head whispered. *You have to swim alongside it.*

I turned my body so that I was parallel with the distant beach and swam for all I was worth. Slowly, I made progress, and the water's draw lessened. Eventually, I was able to move inland, and came ashore on another beach, exhausted but alive.

Gratefully alive.

That shook me out of my malaise. I felt the multiverse coursing in me again, and knew I had to act.

That night, the Dark Monk appeared in my mind with a sword in hand, drawn and ready for battle against the three-headed dragon.

My destiny was still calling to me.

The dawn of blossoming
twilight
awaits
for all who seek.

—From the Nexalistic Revolutionary Front (NRF) Documents by Nathan T. Stanfield (NTS) a.k.a. Steven Kubacki, 1978

* * *

Until then, I hadn't dared to contact anyone, not even my co-conspirators. I trusted that they were busy building the Right Arm of our great revolutionary movement and were having more success than I was with the Left. Paul and Walter were about to graduate from Hope and Calvin respectively, and I needed to talk with them before they left for parts unknown.

One night, I snuck into an empty vacation bungalow and without permission used their phone to call Walter.

He was not happy to hear from me. If anything, his response was paranoid.

This was the first I'd heard about what had happened after my disappearance—how the police had sent helicopters and questioned everyone I knew. Walter said that James was sure that he was still being watched, if not by the police, then by the private investigator my family had hired. James told him that the FBI might even be involved. Walter, not surprisingly, was terrified that he was going to be arrested at any moment.

Richard had been so distraught at my apparent death that Walter and Paul had decided not to tell him about the conspiracy. He'd returned to Atlanta convinced that I was gone, and he'd enrolled in graduate school somewhere in Wisconsin. He told everyone he was going to become a fiction writer.

The NRF, according to Walter, was hanging by a thread. It was a make-or-break moment. If we lost Richard, along with his rich and well-connected family, our vision of supplanting the head of an empire with an NRF agent seemed all but lost. Fiction writers didn't become world leaders.

The dire news was what I needed to jolt myself into action. The NRF was mostly my vision, and only I could stop it from crumbling. Trusting Paul and Walter to handle Richard's entry into our plans had been a mistake.

"I'll go to Wisconsin myself," I told Walter, and then asked him to wire me enough money for a plane ticket. "The revolution is on."

***

In the energy shell, shades of light pierce me. They open my body of light, which I have used to maintain a sense of identity. The opening or slicing can be interpreted as surgery, but it is not. It has a quality of loving kindness. I realize the Others are pouring symphonies of information into me. I think these are complex sets of photons and light waves, what science might now term quantum algorithms. The transdimensional information of each Steven is activated like DNA strands by physical, energetic, dimensional, karmic, and other unknown catalysts.

But more importantly, the color light pouring into this Steven of Light liberates each possible self from other manifestations of me—myriad others, each with their own timelines (or past lives) and other dimensions, but along with them, there are also Stevens of Darkness.

Which ones are activated and transferred by quantum entanglement to my earthly Steven and Nathan aspects is not clear. Without the liberation of the dark Stevens, the Stevens of Light will not be able to influence them or the other darknesses to which they are connected. They will remain hidden within, alone and frightened, and thereby continue the destructive and chaotic darknesses to which they are committed.

Chapter 8

A MOTHER'S INTUITION

March 8, 1978

Dear James:

Some time has passed, and I have been able to gather my wits about me to further assure myself that Steven is, somehow, somewhere, alive. I know this has no apparent reasonable basis, but at least until all the questions have been answered to my satisfaction, I find some peace or at least a "holding action" on my feelings. Your very traumatic experience, along with ours, I hope has now been somewhat eased also . . .

I'm trying my best to understand this whole series of very perplexing and trying events and am still unable to get a semblance of coherence for myself out of everything. Perhaps you can and will help me. My appreciation will be unending.

Sincerely,
Irene Pegg

P.S. I hope you have resumed your classes and are doing well so that you will get your degree in May.

* * *

Mr. George Randolf of the Randolf Investigative Services, Detroit, Michigan, stopped at the South Haven Post at 11:30 a.m. in reference to this complaint. He has been hired by Steven Kubacki's brother, John Kubacki of Massachusetts, to try and find Steven. John Kubacki does not believe his brother drowned, but believes he left the area, possibly to Germany. He has a passport and has been to Germany before. Also if he went, he would have flown by Icelandic Airlines out of Chicago, Illinois. He also dropped off copies of some letters and Steven's telephone statement for January and February 1978.

—From the South Haven, MI, police file investigating the disappearance of Steven Kubacki, March 22, 1978

* * *

I have lost my hiking boots and knife.

I have lost you. The rhythm of verses is a hairy man's noose, which you have unaware slipped around your neck. In the last analysis, bullets cannot pierce me, nonetheless they can kill me, I leave it up to you.

My doom approaches — will I or will I not be apprehended by the agents?

—From the Nexalistic Revolutionary Front (NRF) Documents by Nathan T. Stanfield (NTS) a.k.a. Steven Kubacki, 1978

* * *

Walter's wire transfer came through a few days later, and I once more boarded an airplane and flew across an ocean. On the long trip from Hawaii to San Francisco, there were no beautiful stewardesses to flirt with, and I found myself with plenty of time to consider what Walter had told me about the ongoing search for Steven Kubacki.

While I thought James was being overly paranoid to think he was being watched or recorded, I wasn't all that surprised to know that my mother was pushing for answers and not letting the case die. Irene Pegg was a force—the embodiment of a mother's relentless love, worry, and deep intuition all rolled into one.

A woman's intuition is a powerful thing, especially a mother's. When I was in Massachusetts for Christmas, just before the disappearance, I could tell she knew something was going on. She kept watching me, asking questions about my friends, my plans. I'd tried to remain aloof, keep my mind from anchoring anywhere she could follow, but I don't think doing so made my lying more convincing. I considered that she might have learned to spot the signs, become adept at reading my subtitles, no matter how protected by detachment I may have thought myself.

Unfortunately, men have been making a habit out of ignoring and deriding female intuition for eons.

She'd never felt safe where I was concerned—partly because of the death of my older brother, and partly because of my own proclivity for calamity. It started with my birth—my mother had a serious case of pneumonia, and so the doctors whisked me away as soon as I was born, and she wasn't able to hold me in her arms for six weeks.

At six months old, I'd succumbed to a fever and nearly died. A couple of years later, as a toddler, I climbed onto a third story window ledge, evading my mother's desperate hands. I heard the story many times about how I laughed with delight as I teetered and crawled on the edge of the deadly precipice until my mother could grab me from the next window. In the years that followed, there were hernias, broken bones, and lots of truancies and unexplained absences.

Then, of course, there was my last unexplained long absence from college, just two years before.

There was a reason my mother had her eye on James.

* * *

Not long after we met, James and I had spontaneously decided that we'd had enough of Hoax College, and so one day we just left without telling anyone. We would learn more from the world, we decided, than from some educational system controlled by the people we despised. We had grand plans to circle the globe, first flying to Belgium, where James' mother lived, and then traveling east through the communist territories behind the Iron Curtain, the Middle East, the Steppe, China, and finally to Japan, the Land of the Rising Sun.

It was wildly ambitious, and it fell apart almost immediately: first, because we had no money for plane tickets.

I convinced James to hitchhike to Atlanta, where Richard had returned after his year in Paris. We almost didn't make it; we were arrested for hitchhiking and spent a couple of days in a county jail. When we eventually arrived in Georgia, we were in good spirits, but looked worse for wear when we knocked, unannounced and uninvited, on Richard's door.

I soon discovered that my friend had become more serious since our days in Europe. He declined to join our adventure—he didn't seem to like James very much for some reason—but his generous nature prevailed, and he let us stay in his apartment rent free while we looked for work.

James got a job at a gas station, and I was hired to serve food in a diner that I later discovered was owned by Christians. It was like discovering Hope College's religious roots all over again. But we kept at it for a few weeks, until finally I cracked. I couldn't forget what I'd seen on my first LSD trip, when I saw the Christian proselytizing under the lamppost as a puppet. Now I was surrounded by puppets like that for eight hours a day. I just couldn't take it. The money was good, but these people were delusional, blessing the mashed potatoes, singing hymns while they washed dishes.

I finally cracked. In a fit of mutual lust, the boss's daughter and I entangled our bodies in the dry storage walk-in. We were half-naked when they caught us. Had it been the 1600s, they would have burned me at the stake. Luckily, they just cut me a check and said they'd pray for my soul.

When I told James, he let out a huge sigh of relief. He was ready to get the hell out of the South. He and Richard were butting heads, and our housing was tenuous. I didn't want him to lose interest in our plan, though, so I suggested we make our way to Massachusetts.

Twelve days later, my father pulled into the driveway of his home to discover me sitting on his doorstep. He was more relieved than surprised, because unbeknownst to me, Hope College had noticed my absence and had been calling my mother for several weeks, asking her about my whereabouts. Of course, she had no idea where I was. We hadn't bothered to tell a single soul of our plan to drop out, simply vanishing into the night like runaways. It hadn't even occurred to me to call my parents in all of the weeks we'd spent in Georgia.

So yes, James and I had planted seeds of suspicion in my parents, and my mother's intuitive worry had watered and nurtured them. I later discovered that from the first week when she was at Hope in Holland, Michigan, while everyone else was searching the frozen lake, she was taking inventory in my apartment, noticing details: Why were there cards missing from the wallet I'd left in my backpack? Why did I have such a strange, handwritten will? Why did I still seem to trust James so much?

Reading through my mother's notes, I see how much she saw. "Why wasn't James and father investigated—too powerful?" She asked the private detective in one of her many letters to him:

"Investigate [them] thoroughly. It appears James is not telling all he knows about anything."

Later, she mentions, "James was visibly upset when I was there—yet less than a week later is surly, cold, and gives the appearance of being totally uncaring. Did he put on a good act?... Who emptied out Steve's wallet? What was taken out?? For a routine ski trip over the dunes, he certainly would not empty a wallet. This is apparent by the way a billfold shapes itself over the items inside—it was not in this shape when I saw it, indicating many things missing."

* * *

James and I stayed at my father's house for a month while I worked in a pickle factory to make enough money for travel.

James seemed to have lost interest in the working-class life; he stayed in the house during that time, eating my father's food and drinking his beer without contributing much. My mother, especially, made it clear that she didn't trust him. On Christmas Eve, while my family was milling about and James was opening gifts that they'd all thoughtfully bought for him, she pulled me aside and told me that someday soon, he would abandon me.

And of course, she was right.

In January, we finally flew to Europe to begin our journey to the east. As soon as we arrived, James seemed to wilt. He became a different person—less confident, more nervous, almost jumpy. Almost apologetically, he took me to the town where his mother lived. It was there I discovered that James wasn't just well-to-do; he was filthy rich. We were met at the train station by a driver wearing a tuxedo, hat, driving gloves—the works. He took us to an estate that reminded me of the baron's house in *The Sound of Music*—ornate sandstone, complete with terraces and pillars, overlooking sweeping lawns and a view of a river. James' mother, it turned out, had married a man whose family name was as old as the vineyards that wreathed the countryside. On those lands, there were the spirits of generations of wealth—bloodlines of unchangeable, permanent power.

I wasn't just an outsider here. I was a trespasser.

James' mother certainly thought so, even as I called on all of my Deerfield Academy training in proper upper-crust etiquette. I knew which spoon was the soup spoon, and that there was no such thing as finger food. But it wasn't enough.

"Pierre qui roule n'amasse pas mousse," she told her son that night, right in front of me.

A rolling stone gathers no moss.

To her, moss meant money. Permanence meant power. And a vagabond American like me would never acquire either.

I kept trying to be Zen, to go with the flow. But as days stretched into weeks, James started losing interest in the plan. He'd say, "Maybe we should stay here another week," or "You know, the Middle East is a very ugly place." That house, that money, and his mother's heavy hand all got to him. They wore him down.

I had to get out of there.

That evening, I announced that I would go to Freiburg to visit old friends for a few days. James looked concerned but said nothing. His mother rose from the head of the table and pressed a handful of bills into my palm.

"*Bon voyage*, Steven Kubacki."

* * *

We are the frontier. The frontier reaffirms our fragility, dispels attitudes of immortality, and purges us of our egocentricity. For on the frontier death is imminent; there is not time to bullshit around; life is intense. . .

—From the Nexalistic Revolutionary Front (NRF)
Documents by Nathan T. Stanfield (NTS)
a.k.a. Steven Kubacki, 1978

* * *

I left the chateau in such a hurry I didn't even pack a raincoat, and I arrived in Germany drenched by icy sleet, feeling as if I'd escaped something. My bravado was gone.

Using the last of the money James' mother had given me, I rented a room at a cheap hotel not far from the University of Freiburg. The next day, I called James. I already regretted leaving him, imagining the incredible pressure he was under. In such a setting, it would be hard for him to make his own choices. I needed him to know that I still wanted to travel east with him, that I didn't hold his pedigree against him.

In fact, things were worse than I thought. I dialed the number for the mansion, where a servant answered and told me to wait. Then, instead of James' familiar voice, I heard his mother.

Her son was no longer in the country, she told me without even saying hello. She said he'd "finally listened to reason" and had returned to Hope, uncoupling himself from "whatever plans" we had made.

Her words struck me like physical blows. I let the phone slip from my fingers, lost in the midst of a sudden realization that I was alone, abandoned again.

Much, much later, I found out that the truth was much more complicated. James called me while he was on an acid trip and confessed that his mother had conspired against us both. Hours after I'd left for Freiburg, she gave him a letter from the Belgian government that had arrived some time before. Because he was a Belgian citizen through his mother, James said, the government demanded that he meet his requirement to enlist in the armed services. However, she coolly reminded him, the United States didn't permit its citizens to undergo military training from different countries, and so the American citizenship he'd received through his father was at risk. He was in a catch-22 of sorts.

James told me he'd "struck an impulsive deal with the devil." He agreed that if his mother's aristocratic husband could arrange it so that James would retain his dual citizenship without military service, he would do as they wished and return to Hope to complete his studies. The whole affair had been chaotic, and he was on an airplane headed back to Michigan by the end of the day. Only when his feet touched American tarmac, James said, did he realize that he had left me behind.

He pled with me from the pit of his soul, begging for my forgiveness. And I offered it, of course. I was grateful to have an explanation, but I doubted whether he could remain a best friend.

But that was far in the future. In Freiburg, all I knew was that I was alone.

* * *

I was in a terrible state of mind, barely aware of anything. Needed to hear a soothing voice, I called my mother from a postal phone service, but I could not bring myself to tell her the truth. Instead, I said everything was great and that James and I were staying in Germany for a few days before setting out on our adventure.

My mother questioned me several times, asking repeatedly if everything was all right. I'm sure my voice did not come across with the usual Steven bravado. At the end of our brief conversation, she stated emphatically that if I was ever in any kind of difficulty, she would send me fare for a plane ticket home. It was never easy to lie to her.

It was snowing and very cold, and after we hung up, I wandered the streets of Freiburg for hours. I thought about disappearing into the Black Forest. I'd heard stories about strange and magical things that happened there.

Instead, I pulled myself together and sought the only friend I thought might still be there for me. I called the administrator of the university and asked for a particular schedule. I then went to a café with a view of the street.

At half past six, Professor Astrid Leinbach strolled past the café window, right on schedule. I still remember that she wore a peacoat of emerald green and a red scarf to cover her hair.

The year before, when I was a student at Freiburg, I'd had an affair with Astrid. She was a glamorous, brainy, aloof goddess whose classes dug deep into philosophy and modern political history. She had a huge house where she hosted parties full of radicals, political intellectuals, and hardcore anti-capitalists and anti-imperialists—people who wanted to tear down the very society she had built her life around. Her students loved her, and more than a few, like me, were in love with her. Of all of them, she had chosen me.

As I watched her through the window, I remembered the day just before Christmas break when our choices had become obvious. Rain fell in icy sheets as my fellow classmates filed into the building for Astrid's German lecture. Instead of going in, I circled the perimeter, counting the windows on the fourth floor until I found the one where Astrid would be teaching. I groped the seams between the granite rocks and started to climb. Hand over hand, I scaled the side of the building like a thrill-seeking junkie or an insane thief. By the time I reached the top floor, some thirteen meters above the snow-covered concrete, I was soaked to the bone and charged with adrenaline.

I could see Astrid inside the classroom, her back to the window as she lectured the class. I pressed myself against the floor-to-ceiling window and smiled as big as I could. Finally, someone—a classmate named Jenny—saw me and screamed, practically falling out of her chair. Everyone else jumped up and started pointing, and the room turned into chaos. Astrid whirled around and ran to the window, sliding it open and yanking me inside into her arms. I could feel her trembling, even though I was the one covered in frozen rain. As she pressed herself against me, I could feel every inch of her body and I knew I was more than her student.

The affair with Astrid lasted the rest of the academic year, and it energized me both physically and intellectually. She introduced me to radical German and French writers, and I convinced her to run naked in the rain on trails next to her house. I hoped she could be the female partner I had been searching for all my life—an equal, my complement. But, alas, while Astrid liked to flirt with radical ideas and lifestyles, in the end she wasn't willing to venture that far out of her gilded cage. We parted at the end of the semester.

If she was at all surprised to see me now, shivering and distraught outside a German café, she made no sign of it. She was polite, but clearly not happy to see me. She sat while I told her my story, and then, without much discussion, came to my hotel. We spent one last night together, but the passion between us was gone.

The next day, Astrid told me that she would make some calls. A few hours later, she found me in the same café and told me she'd found me a room on a local farm run by a pillar of a woman named Dame Banhofer. I could lodge there in exchange for work on the farm. I was too verklempt to come up with anything better, so I went along with it. And Dame Banhofer may have been just what I required in that moment. She saw this wet, skinny, American boy with a broken heart and went to work on me straight away. Every night there was a huge dinner, and no one gave a shit which fork I used to eat my salad or if I wiped my hands on my trousers. I worked in her yard, tilling and digging. Her son Rudolph played blues music on his guitar, and I taught him the English words for the song "Gotta Work for this Damn Lady." He'd laugh as we sang the refrain together: "All day long, for cold soup and dry crackers."

Eventually, I started formally tutoring Rudolph in English, then others on nearby farms and down in the city. It was a peaceful life, and I felt welcomed.

I rode out the remainder of the winter at the farm, tutoring whenever I could to make extra cash to buy books in the city. I read more about Milarepa, the murderer turned Buddhist monk who would influence so much of my experience in Japan. I learned the earliest lessons in how to draw spiritual strength from the dark feelings that swirled within me. Rather than reject anger, sadness, loss, and pain, I used them to dull the edges of my mind made jagged by James' betrayal and smooth my thinking.

I wrote poetry and began to draw with charcoal on the white walls in my room—crescent moons, stars, planets, evergreens, mountains, suns, and other spiritual symbols. My whole life I'd felt alone even when I was with other people. I was always different from them, apart from them. At the Banhofers', it wasn't a big deal, though. We all agreed I was different because I was an American. My otherness was not a byproduct of something dark or tragic. We all just chalked it up to me being a foreigner.

I should mention here, it never occurred to me as months passed to contact my mother again or let her know where I was or that I was safe.

* * *

The rain is falling again in a yellow mist, which a Rhinoceros could never sever. The small sparrow (who lives in the woods) yelps like a cat who thinks he's a dog. Together they follow their ways onto the path of creations unforeseen. Somewhere I took your hand and grasped a branch of call-to-me-incense that somehow spoke of you as you on a pond floating to a spring.

The rain is falling through your hair, the sky is shining in your eyes — but — the rain is falling, you know, and your clothes are sparkling wet, and our shadows have melted

and we undress the evening

and we reap its darkness

and fall deeper in the rain

—Steven Kubacki, 1976

* * *

Things went smoothly until one afternoon in late April when I borrowed Dame Banhofer's bicycle to go into the city to buy a new book. I had read Milarepa from front to back innumerable times and was in desperate need of a change. In fact, I longed for change in more ways than that. Life on the farm had begun to feel routine—boring, even. It lacked spontaneity and intrigue. But most importantly, it lacked anyone of my own age and the opposite sex.

Cresting one of the many bridges that span the lesser tributaries of the mighty Dreisam River, I spotted another cyclist heading my way. When our paths crossed, we then each skidded to a halt.

It was Suzanne, a woman I'd seen several times since I arrived in Freiburg. Our meetings were always brief but seemed to carry the weight of synchronicity, and I was intrigued—more than intrigued.

That day on the bridge, she looked just as beautiful and enchanting as every other time I'd accidentally run into her. She hugged me, and I felt like she was casting a spell. Later, she told me she thought I was doing the same thing. She called me a *magier*—a wizard or mage.

The time had come to shake things up again, and Suzanne was the answer. We were almost immediately inseparable. Unfortunately, Dame Banhofer had a strict no-girls-allowed policy in her house, so I collected my stuff and moved out. Suzanne and I slept every night in a tent I set up on another farm.

She brought dozens of oversized modern art books that we piled inside the tent until there was barely enough room to lay next to each other. I was enthralled by her energy and intelligence. We spent weeks exploring the Black Forest, discovering caves and grottos where strange mushrooms grew. Suzanne was an expert mushroom hunter—she knew exactly which kind to pick to send you on a trip like you couldn't believe.

Suzanne was spontaneous, which I appreciated. But it could be a double-edged sword. I was feeling very Zen, sitting in the forest for hours, listening for lost cattle or to the inhalations and exhalations of the trees. But Suzanne got bored easily—and before I knew it—she was gone: out of my tent, out of my life. It was only decades later that I found out that she moved to Berlin, became a nurse, married a doctor, and became a very traditional middle-class mother.

* * *

Suzanne's abandonment, so soon after James', was a lot to carry, and I didn't take it very well. If I hadn't been practicing Zen, it would have broken me. It almost did. The day I realized she wasn't coming back, I went out into the woods near our tent and picked the hallucinogenic mushrooms that Suzanne had showed me. I started eating them, more than I'd ever taken before, more than a human should probably take. I spent the next week or longer alone in the forest, moving from one reality to another—moving *through* them.

I do not escape, but I do get very, very lost. I draw on rock walls and write incomprehensible poetry. I tear pages from the art books Suzanne had left behind and rearrange them into collages that pull me into their multifaceted geometries, invading my surroundings with strange shapes. The boundaries between greens, browns, and other earth tones blur and mix, bleeding into the trees and landscapes. Vague pools of nondescript forms emerge and evaporate so that all distinctiveness become secondary.

I am a monk, running barefoot, chanting in a language I do not know on snowy paths in high mountains with glaciers.

I stand in a jungle, swaying in a pyramid-shaped stone hut, drumming, rattling, pulling ugly insect forms out of a woman lying on the grass mat with dark stones on her body. There are other people lined up outside.

I see a drunk man in an alley, surrounded by trash, shivering with a face like mine, but gaunt and emaciated.

I feel someone touching me gently on my shoulder. I turn around and see nothing. A darkness seems to be covering me. The darkness becomes porous with myriad points of light. The light penetrates, and I see a colored light in the shape of a body.

I was simultaneously elated, awed, but terribly frightened. The time came when I just wanted to be myself again. But I couldn't—I'd lost control.

The only thing that saved me, ironically, was becoming so deathly sick that I almost died. Alone in my tent, deep in the Black Forest, I was pulled from my interdimensional excursions by a powerful fever caused by an infected tick bite.

When the fever did not break for a week, I dragged myself to a doctor, who carved into my skin and removed the infected area. Still, the infection continued to spread, and soon my brain began to simmer like a stew. Angry boils broke out all over my body, causing me incomprehensible pain. In desperation, I made my way to the Banhofers'. Dame Banhofer took one look at the half-crazed American and promptly called my mother.

I hardly remember my flight home from Germany. I was still so sick and feverish that they quarantined me in the back of the plane. I had broken free from nonreality, but my mind was wide open—gaping, even. My body was in deep trouble.

My mother met me on the tarmac at Connecticut's Bradley International Airport during a thunderstorm. I have no idea how she convinced the airline to let her go outside like that. My first clear memory for months is feeling her wrap me in an embrace heavy with distress.

Over the months that followed, she nursed me back to physical health and convinced me to return to Hope to finish my degree. I reluctantly agreed, mostly to make her happy, but also because James was there, and we had somewhat reconciled.

She watched me more closely after that adventure.

Less than two years later, I vanished again. Was it any wonder that she would be suspicious? She knew that I was prone to act impulsively, to do things outside the norm, and to disappear.

I recently read some of her notes and journal entries from that time, and a phrase jumps out at me: "Is he now living the life of a wanderer/sorcerer?"

She was so much closer to the truth than she knew.

* * *

April 11, 1978

Mr. George Randolph
Randolph Investigatory Services

Dear Mr. Randolph,

I wish to thank you for your efforts in attempting to find new factual evidence/information (re: the list of specific, as yet unanswered questions) that my brother Steven met with foul play or that there were other unknown circumstances regarding his disappearance.

Since, in both your conversations with me and with my Mother, you have been unable to find new evidence to substantiate or warrant further investigation, we wish to close this case. Please send a report as soon as possible.

Most or all of the information you have been able to solicit is pretty much hearsay, imprudent observations and unsophisticated opinions of people not even necessarily acquainted or close to Steven.

We feel that this is most deleterious to both Steven's character and reputation, especially since neither he nor his family have any recourse to refute any or all of this. We are, therefore, satisfied that the State Police did and are doing a thorough investigation and nothing is to be gained by further outside investigation.

Perhaps it was not stressed at the time you were hired (more understood by us), but all information, documented or otherwise, is to be kept strictly confidential.

Sincerely yours,

John J. Kubacki, Jr.

* * *

I find it very difficult to understand why it appears to me at least that no one understands why I have (as John J calls it) an obsession to find Steven. To me, in every respect it is a normal inclination... They look at me questioningly — afraid to say what they are thinking — looking so intently to see my reaction. To me it is plain and simple — do all I can to find my son. I feel I cannot talk to anyone about him anymore — is it that they are trying to forget, and I am trying to find him and not forget anything? Am I being paranoid or are they? I'm a pretty rational person and can think things out fairly well — so what's wrong, or am I not what I think I am? The attitude toward me by my family makes me wonder!

—From the letters of Irene Pegg, June 1978

Chapter 9
BACK IN THE USA

Nathan,

As the Left Arm and coordinator of illegitimate operations, you must also be concerned with the nature of your organization. It must have legitimate claims. It cannot be wholly clandestine but must imbibe sprinklings of the acceptable. This is done via the Robin Hood method. Guerilla activities must be aimed at specific targets. Civilians are to remain unharmed. . . Financial and industrial targets are especially productive. . . Maintenance of an even remotely condoning populace is an absolute necessity. . .

Assassinate only hated leaders. Do not terrorize civilians. Do not pursue ransom policies. . . We are at the threshold.

—Walter, 1978

* * *

From Mexico City to Osaka to Hawaii and now in San Francisco, I had surely gotten around, I chuckled to think. I went directly from the San Francisco airport to the Greyhound bus terminal and headed east toward Madison, Wisconsin, where Richard lived and wrote in ignorance of all that was coming his way.

I wasn't actually worried about what I would say to him. The mission and goal of the NRF, I was sure, would speak for itself.

Once he understood the importance of what I had done, all would be forgiven, and the future president would be back on track.

The bus took a circuitous route, winding south through Arizona and New Mexico, where the sun was relentless, before turning north. I passed three long, hot days by building out the NRF papers, writing for hours about centralization and decentralization in political economics. Centralization in authoritarian governments or corporations, I argued, always led to economic catastrophes and reduction in economic ecosystem diversity. Decentralization of economic wealth and political power, therefore, would be essential to freedom, creativity, and the balance of individual and social interests. The words flowed onto my notebook pages as if I'd always known them, or did I draw from a vaguely remembered experience? Another divergence with everyday reality.

Outside the bus, the countryside morphed and changed, and I had visions of running and chanting for endless miles on footpaths in glaciated mountains. This, too, felt familiar. I had been among these Himalayan spires before this timeline. But just as the peak was within reach, I felt an impenetrable darkness cloud my mind. Drawn to its depths, I heard the Dark Monk asking, "How is Steven doing on the lake?" I sensed the Dark Monk didn't care. He asked so I would feel alone, more disconnected from Steven, and so more dependent on him.

* * *

People in power can become bureaucratic slobs when they are not considered expendable. They become intrinsic and all too vital to those they have bamboozled, including themselves. Appropriately, we designate them as cowards who pander to a self-image of historical success and security with little or no self-sacrifice. In doing so, they become known as so-called great and powerful leaders. . . They sit in their offices or behind the front lines and command without ever taking any risks or jeopardizing their status. Little do they realize that this ignoble performance transforms them into the very oppressors and bigots they once despised. No man is to retain his position of power and influence for any extended period, hence a perpetual reshuffling of men as agents of power is requisite. . . Please, no more Lenins and elite party machines. Please, no more Maos and the tyranny of emulation. . .

—From the Nexalistic Revolutionary Front (NRF)
Documents by Nathan T. Stanfield (NTS)
a.k.a. Steven Kubacki, 1978

* * *

Finally, after more stops and starts than I could count, the bus rattled into the depot in Madison. As I gathered my things, I noticed a beautiful but oddly striking woman a few rows ahead of me. Had she been there the whole time? Something about the way her dark hair—oddly cut, perhaps with her own scissors—covered her eyes and shielded her unconventionally pretty face gave off an aura of mystery. I felt the wave of otherness radiating from her, and I knew that she, too, was hiding in plain sight, visible only to those with the will and means to see her.

In an instant I forgot about Richard. Not forgot, exactly, but I was captivated by this young woman in hiking boots and a knee-length skirt. She walked like she knew where she was going, and all I could do was follow her.

I dubbed her the Lone Woman. I believed her a fellow fugitive.

I trailed the Lone Woman to a colorful neighborhood full of college students and artists. Every now and then, she glanced back at me. She felt my presence just as I felt hers. Eventually, she ducked into a coffee shop and vanished amongst the crowds packed in for a poetry reading.

I would not be deterred. I found an open table near the door. I was working up the courage to dive into the people, to find her, to introduce myself, to discover her. Before I could do any of that, she appeared again and sat down across from me. Without even saying hello, she asked why I was following her.

When people are hiding, they don't want to be noticed. Yet I saw her, and now she saw me. And there was only one thing to do.

I told her everything.

Yes, everything.

The NRF, my death, alternative timelines, and multiverse selves. It was a total act of faith, or perhaps desperation. But I was sure this woman was important, would be important, might be the most important of us all. I felt the tug of the universe, and maybe a generous dose of magical thinking.

The only thing I didn't share was my actual name. I told her I was Nathan. She told me I reminded her of a combination of Holden Caulfield in *Catcher in the Rye* and Travis Bickle from *Taxi Driver*.

Her name was Natalie. I told her I would always call her the Lone Woman.

* * *

A lone woman
stands alone
and those who stand
wither
are alone
Her icy hands
touch ice
and those who walk
wither
see ice

—From the Nexalistic Revolutionary Front (NRF)
Documents by Nathan T. Stanfield (NTS)
a.k.a. Steven Kubacki, 1978

* * *

We spent the entire afternoon talking in the coffee shop, interrupted occasionally by the annoyingly persistent owner, who was evidently an old friend of Natalie's. Our conversation was wide-ranging and lithe, and I was compelled by her nuanced political views and knowledge of fine art, especially opera. She carried mystery, shared no personal stories, but it was clear she'd traveled the world.

At the same time, she embraced the uncertainty, mystery, and disorder that defined me.

We parted ways at dusk, assured that our paths would cross again. I struck off up the street with a bounce in my step, while Natalie stayed at the coffee shop to catch up with her friend.

It was past nightfall when I found Richard's house, and for the first time all day, I felt a pang of apprehension. I wasn't totally immune to James' paranoia.

How does one know if they're being watched? If a house is being watched? I deliberately walked past Richard's building, keeping my collar turned up to hide my face. I scanned the cars parked along the street, looking for the telltale glow of a cigarette, the paunch and drooping moustache of the man James had described to Walter, a chain-smoking guy in a rumpled suit. I almost laughed at the surreal nature of the moment. Was I being a cliché, or looking for one?

The cars facing Richard's door were all empty, so I gathered my courage and went to the door. I was a ghost in the flesh, haunted by the memory of a life that was and was not mine.

I hadn't actually seen Richard since James and I had stayed with him two years before in our ill-fated attempt to drop out of Hoax College. Walter told me about Richard's later trip to my father's house after I disappeared to comfort my parents. My mind tickled the edge of imagining what he'd been through, but I put the thought aside. I called on the Dark Monk.

Ruthless compassion over empathy.

I knocked on the door and waited, and then Richard was there, his eyes like saucers. He grabbed me, shook me a little, like he was making sure I was real. Then we were in the kitchen, and I was telling him over and over again, "Yes, it really is me. Yes, I really am alive."

The night becomes a blur after that. I remember Richard asking if I was hungry, and when I said I hadn't eaten in a while, pouring me a giant glass of beer. We drank and laughed. Richard wasn't angry at my deception. It was more like he was like a kid on Christmas who'd just caught Santa stuffing the stockings.

Eventually the giddiness wore off and Richard got serious. "But why?" he asked. "Why fake your death?"

And so I told the story for the second time that day—the NRF, the three-headed dragon, the way that we could change the world and make things right.

I don't know what I expected from him, but he was so unsurprised that I was almost insulted.

"Of course you faked your own death to start a revolution," was all he said that night.

"You're Steven Fucking Kubacki."

* * *

A memo to the NRF:

Richard and I have established the first Commando Marathon Unit, whose specialties lie in its very abilities of long-distance endurance, commending to us the capability to strike swiftly and unexpectantly from long, unthinkable (to our enemy impossible) distances against his positions.

a marathon
sleep the night before
and you can run
like the wind

We are training generally at night to improve our twilight awareness, for as we all realize, most assaultive operations, for purposes of maximizing security and feasibility while minimizing casualties, will be conducted in the dark hours of the day. . .

I would like to add at this juncture that physical fitness is of the utmost importance to all.

Any of us and all of us (sooner or later) will be called upon to die. . .

—From the Nexalistic Revolutionary Front (NRF)
Documents by Nathan T. Stanfield (NTS)
a.k.a. Steven Kubacki, 1978

* * *

That was all I told Richard that night. I didn't describe the role I'd saved for him in the Right Arm or tell him about the visions and multiverse experiences that drove me now. Richard had similar views on the role of visions, connections with the unseen, and drawing power and knowledge from other realities, so I wasn't worried about his reaction to those experiences. But I knew he needed to get on board on his own, and that his commitment would be deeper and stronger if he felt like it came from within, and so it should. All I needed to do was stay close and wait for his natural magnanimousness to bring him to the knowledge that the NRF and its mission were necessary not only for world change, but for him personally.

I suggested that I stay with him for a while as I continued my physical training, because no one would look for me in Madison, Wisconsin. I described the schedule I'd learned from the warrior monks in Japan and suggested I wanted something similar here, only without the outside efforts to control me.

The idea of intense physical and mental conditioning intrigued Richard, who had run marathons in the past and was already training for another. He not only welcomed me to stay, rent free, in his apartment, but also asked to train with me. It was everything I'd hoped for.

We started running three miles each morning before breakfast and added workouts in almost every free hour between his classes. We trained like Zen martial artists: running, drilling, pushing one another to go farther, try harder.

As weeks passed and our physical and mental tiredness intensified, the norms of our morality and expected behavior weakened. We drove ourselves hard, and the more we ran, the more we lucidly perceived the trees and the darkness itself.

We talked for hours, and the NRF became more real. Richard's passion for the grandiose mission gave me an audience to weave the narrative, tying our revolution to the broader history of revolution and utopias. We were anarcho-syndicalists rising against fascist Franco in Spain, we were Pancho Villa in Mexico, we were Republicans in Rome.

While Richard was in class, I walked the streets of Madison, often with Natalie, or wrote essays and letters about our mission. My words came out like prophecy—albeit prophecy tempered with biting sarcasm, mysticism, poetry, and free-associative ramblings.

Of course, when we weren't plotting and scheming the overthrow of corrupt systems, we were also normal young American men who contradicted their own anti-establishment ideals, devouring hamburgers and French fries, peeing in toilets, watching MLB (Major

League Baseball), and buying Nike running shoes. Mundaneness penetrated our lives, balancing out the radical and frightening unknown we claimed to embrace. We justified this by discussing the importance of being grounded and connected to society. How could we be understood and accepted by those we were supposed to save without significant acculturation and roots in normative society? Without common social rituals and actions, we would be weird, we said, and few would follow us.

Our revolution could not be *too* revolutionary if it was to succeed.

* * *

May 1978

Dear Paul,

Gosh, you're the only "nice guy" we've got, besides me — when I'm in one of my pathological writer moods. Look, why don't we all form a commune on some good Kansas pasture and crawl on all fours and graze all day . . . then flit off to all corners of the world? Pervasive power dreaming seeping into behavior, until friends crawl at our feet and beg for weapons!

I write to declare that I belong irrevocably to the Left Arm.

Richard

* * *

I think we both loved it at first. Richard thrived on the energy that was building between us. Our intensity poured over into every aspect of life. His novel writing improved, and I could see how his creative writing now would make him a captivating public speaker when he became a charismatic politician. He had a gift with words and a brilliant mind.

Our zeal filled the voids of our rather regimented life. We kept pressure on each other. Richard's intensity forced me to step up. Leading the Left Arm by myself had been much lonelier than I'd expected. Richard offered the mutual reinforcement that a social person like me needed for true commitment. He also provided a safe address from where I could communicate with the rest of the NRF via letter. Paul, especially, became a prolific pen pal as he approached graduation and considered his choices for seminary. Where would he best serve the Right Arm?

The only fly in the ointment, if there was one, was Walter's seeming reticence to finance our efforts. We ran through Richard's money quickly, an allowance from his rich father more than enough for one, but not sufficient for two young and hungry men. To us, it did not matter that Walter was still a college student himself, finishing his last semester at Calvin College. He was supposed to be our billionaire financier. Where was his commitment to the Left Arm?

My lingering grudge against Walter for relying on Alex Linke, who had acquired a car that didn't work on the day of the disappearance, rose back to the surface, and I was quick to criticize and doubt him. Here was a friend wholly committed to and driven by our ideas when we were together at Calvin College or Hope, but could I trust him when I was out of sight? Had he encouraged my disappearance just to get rid of me and my wild ideas, to get all this out of his life so he could marry a good Christian girl and hang out with conservative finance execs? Unfairly, I demanded frequent reassurance of his commitment, which he easily offered, but at times I deemed his responses not ardent enough—he could be a master at lying about anything, even the most trivial of things.

When Richard's semester ended in June, we decided to take the NRF's financial concerns—as well as our own—into our own hands. Richard's father owned several warehouses by the ocean in Charleston, and he wanted help to run them through the busy summer season. We decided to spend the summer in the South, building both the coffers and the vision of the NRF.

We stopped in Atlanta on the way to spend a few days with Richard's family. Neither of us considered it a risk, since I hadn't met them the last time I was in Atlanta with James. Still, though, Richard had been devastated by his friend Steven's disappearance not that many months ago, and it was entirely possible his parents had seen media stories since then. To not even discuss preparing a cover story would be a wild risk based in magical thinking.

But it worked. I met Richard's parents as Nathan, a Wisconsin friend as close to Richard as a long-lost brother. They opened their arms in welcome. Steven stayed lost on Lake Michigan.

After a few days, we continued on to Charleston and the busy warehouse on the waterfront. Richard and I worked during the day in the warehouse, sweating like pigs in the South Carolina heat. At night, we'd do our drills and talk NRF strategy. Some evenings we got tickets to see the Atlanta Braves and see some of our favorite baseball heroes out on the field.

I could see that Richard was becoming zealous, so much so that he sometimes accused me, the one who'd faked his own death, of not taking the revolution seriously enough. He was committed—

ready to die for the cause, for his chosen path in the Right Arm. My ambivalence about taking on the darkness of the Left Arm frustrated him and me.

* * *

At the end of the summer, we drove straight back to Wisconsin, taking turns driving for the eighteen-hour trip. Richard spent the time conceptualizing the various important roles he would play in the revolution, but I had other things on my mind—specifically, Natalie's dark hair, dark eyes, and wicked smile. I'd missed her terribly over the summer and had written her letters that she never answered.

She'd gotten under my skin in just a few weeks, which was particularly confusing because I'd never made a move. I'd never even kissed her. It wasn't like me to be so inhibited with a woman, but the Lone Woman was like no one else I'd ever known.

I'd never trusted what the universe offered in the way of female companionship. Most women I met didn't spark my interest, not because they weren't amazing in their own way, but because I didn't feel an intense resonance with them. When one emerged—like Astrid, the professor at Freiburg—I was more chicken than intuitive ninja. If I'm honest, all of my early experiences happened because the woman made the first move. But as Nathan, my experience was different. I trusted and allowed the attraction to guide me.

With Natalie, I pictured Izumi and the things she'd taught me, and I dreamed of sharing that with her. Paradoxically, the more Richard talked, the more I avoided actions and suppressed thoughts about the revolution.

As soon as we got back, I left Richard at the house and went to the coffee shop where I'd first met Natalie, and where she still lived in an apartment above the kitchen. This was where I always found her. I didn't linger on the idea that she never came looking for me, had no idea where I lived, had never met Richard. She was hesitant to meet anyone, to share any details. It was all for the best. We were somehow both on the run from our pasts.

I was reassured of Natalie's affection when she greeted me with an embrace. We chatted for hours, catching up after a summer apart. While I had been circumspect in my letters to her, in person I divulged too much, unburdening myself about Richard's growing commitment to the NRF.

The weather that day was balmy and warm, and I still remember the way the sun kissed her shoulders and neck as we left the coffee shop and the watchful glare of its jealous owner. I'd asked Natalie about him, but she was vague with her answers. "An old friend," she assured me again that afternoon, and then pulled out an ornate tin containing four pieces of blotter paper, heavily laced with LSD.

I hadn't taken acid since I was at Hoax College. Yet the day was so beautiful, and Natalie so lovely, that I could not refuse in the end. I felt the urge to access the extraordinary with her, to heal myself or others, to discover profound insights.

We divided the hits and took them on the spot. Willingly I let Natalie take my hand and lead me toward the Madison campus. There, we went into an older building, and then through an unmarked door that led underground. I never asked how she had found the miles of subterranean maintenance tunnels that twisted between buildings and dormitories, critical passages during the cold winter months—or were they built because of the cold war and threat of nuclear annihilation? On the balmy days before classes began, they were deserted, a labyrinth of mist and shadows.

The acid takes hold—the sun, the moon, and stars penetrate the layers of earth and concrete. Distant energies enter our hearts, and I feel each breath submerge me in waves of transcendent possibility. The energy within and without cascades onto our translucent bodies—gentle vibrations shaking our minds with immeasurable cataclysms.

Split into fractalized layers, the ordinary tunnels become tunnels to other tunnels and to other places. I avoid dark openings I feel lead nowhere, or to dark places, and at first Natalie follows. But we are floating on other planes and soon are hopelessly lost in a hallway full of storerooms. In one, Natalie strokes an artifact that resembles a medical machine, though neither of us could imagine what procedure it performs.

In the back of the room is an iron lung or sterilization chamber of some kind, a vast apparatus of tubes and stainless-steel panels. Natalie asks if I want to go inside. I smile. I can't say no to her, of course, and so I step into the silo and offer no resistance as Natalie shuts its heavy door and turns the lock. What little light we have in the room is reduced to nothing at all. LSD can distort time, so what seems forever takes seconds and what seems seconds can take years. I have no idea how long I am in the tube.

In the unending darkness, I am suddenly terrified Natalie might leave me there for eternity. What a trusting fool I am. What a dead fool I will be.

Can a man who is already dead die?

My heart, already wildly erratic, speeds up dangerously, and the limited oxygen in the capsule fades. I must stay calm. I force my breath to slow, my muscles to relax.

In that state of controlled consciousness, I see light penetrate the metal and fill the darkness. It touches my skin and fuses with me, and in that moment, I know Natalie will not harm me or allow harm to visit me. She is tenderness. She is love.

I feel a moment of bliss, of unity with everything. But my peace wakes the Dark Monk from the core of my unraveling ego. In the confined space, he fills me, surrounds me, intimidates me. He ridicules notions such as love, calls it the destroyer of compassionate praxis—the capacity to sacrifice self for the greater good—the very purpose of the NRF—my purpose.

Love, the Dark Monk argues, is the ultimate form of selfishness and small mindedness. It always ends tragically. He pelts me with images of my past failed relationships. This is no longer the time for love. This is the opportunity to bring grand changes into reality.

I weather the onslaught without being moved. The idea of Natalie is too powerful.

Universal love emanates in my mind, pushing back the Dark Monk's attack until Natalie herself, in the flesh, opens the door again. Like a flame without oxygen, the dark energy gradually dwindles, then is snuffed out altogether.

Staring out from the tube, I feel the heartbeat of everything in existence. Specifically, I feel Natalie. All of the possible versions of myself, across the multiverse, have now decohered to become Nathan with Natalie. Another timeline unfolds.

* * *

It's not until much later that I could see all the bombs that were ticking that summer, just waiting to blow up our perfect plans. Lovers and the ardent alike can be dangerous—especially to those to whom they have declared a commitment. They can be rash. They can act impulsively, out of emotion. I was torn in two directions. Walter was withdrawing. And Richard was a tiger, unwilling to let anyone restrict him or allow anyone to get in his way. We were all smart, unpredictable, and dangerous alphas, and though I didn't want to admit it, after six months, the NRF was as fragile as ever.

Chapter 10

THE MEETING

A Memo to the Right Arm from NJS:

Arguments have been summoned from their historical context by the Right Arm and injected into the present to formulate an anachronistic policy. This is a folly I most feared. The Right Arm has allowed itself to be dogmatized by a plan of action, a plan perhaps so iniquitous and wasteful that it may rob us of our best men . . . I do not, nor have I suggested that the Right Arm disband itself or compromise its purpose. I have merely suggested a flexible, future-oriented policy to get its job done, instead of its present policy of inflexibility and homage to historical tyranny . . . Obviously at the present stage all we can do is what we have previously agreed upon, i.e., RJ in politics, WS in business, PM in religion, NJS in the [Left Arm], etc. Our paths are clear at least at the MOMENT.

Memo: PM to the Left Arm:

Fuck you and your burlap French coat with a textbook in one pocket and a bomb in the other! Remember no concessions are possible in the Left Arm, and no revolution lacks its concessions. The Right Arm represents the legitimizing concessions necessary for the diversity of the NRF.

—From the Nexalistic Revolutionary Front (NRF) Documents, 1978

***

That LSD trip was a turning point for me. I realized that I could give it all up for Natalie, who represented the love that permeated existence—that feeling of connection to all possibilities, past, present, and future. I could throw away the NRF and reemerge just for her.

The fuse had been lit.

A few days after my trip in the tunnels, Richard came home with a letter from Walter, and it was full of clippings from the personal ads of local newspapers—*The Dallas Times Herald, The Michigan Daily, The Atlanta Journal-Constitution*, and even a few papers in Europe. They all said essentially the same thing:

STEVEN

I Love You And Need You.

Please Come Home. Call, Anything.

Others Too.

MOMMY

My mother, it seems, had started posting ads in newspapers around the world, anywhere she thought I might be, begging me to come home. It was a long shot at best, an act of desperation undertaken after the spring thaws of Lake Michigan did not deliver a body. She was certain I was alive.

Never underestimate the power of a mother's love.

The ads were extremely hard to look at—especially after my recent brush with love.

Richard noticed my discomfort, but instead of sympathizing, he got agitated and lectured me about the importance of sacrifice and commitment to the cause.

It was too much, all too much. Before I could stop myself, I exploded at him. Where was his sacrifice, I asked. In his comfortable position writing novels, planning a future of comfort within the system? And then I told him about Natalie, about my vision in the tunnels. I told him that I was falling in love.

I remember Richard looked at me for long seconds in silence, in shock. To this point, I hadn't even mentioned Natalie's name to him, despite how close we were. Something had kept me from letting those parts of my world overlap, and now I understood why.

Nothing in the room moved. Richard and I stared at each other. The Dark Monk hovered behind him, mocking me. Pitying me.

And then my friend, the man who was like a brother to me, lost his mind. I'd never seen him so agitated. I've rarely seen anyone in such controlled rage. He yelled and threatened to expose me—call the police, my parents—tell them where I was and what I'd done. He hurled insults, called me a traitor, told me that everyone would hate me and I would go to jail.

As hard as this might be to believe, at the time, the idea that there might be legal consequences to faking my death had never occurred to me. Had I actually done something illegal? I thought about the helicopters, the police, the expense incurred. I backtracked. I wasn't abandoning the NRF, I told Richard. I pledged my commitment to the Left Arm and to the revolution. I tried, as convincingly as I could, to laugh off my feelings for Natalie as a mere fling, something passing and trivial. I pretended it was all a bad joke Richard had fallen for.

He wasn't an idiot, though. We'd spent intense hours together. He knew when I was joking and when I was serious. He believed that Natalie was a serious threat to him and what he dreamed. Instead of backing down, he told me he needed more than my words. He was deeply concerned I didn't have the stuff to lead a revolution.

My mind raced. In that moment, I knew that he was right, that he saw something in me that I didn't—the Stevens who were interested in other timelines, other multiverses, other directions in life. I could feel the pull of interdimensional communing. He was sensing them, too, even if he didn't have the words for it.

Yet those paths were closed to me. I had to be Nathan, the Nathan the NRF demanded.

What would prove my commitment?

"I'll run the marathon with you," I said. Richard had been training to run a marathon in Milwaukee that was a few weeks away. I hadn't planned to join him, since I was technically in hiding, and I wasn't drawn to organized events like that. But this was something important to Richard, and I latched onto it as a way to show him I was still mentally and physically in control.

Richard was skeptical but mollified. We ran the marathon together in the first week of October. His time was much better than mine, but I thought the urgency was behind us. I thought he trusted me again.

I was wrong.

* * *

Saccharine explanations cannot be
a substitute for the
raw honey
of action

—From the Nexalistic Revolutionary Front (NRF)
Documents by Nathan T. Stanfield (NTS)
a.k.a. Steven Kubacki, 1978

I heard you were a budding revolutionary.

I hear that you were reading the classics

Lenin, Mao, Che, DeBray, Marighella,

I heard that you bought a 500-dollar rifle

I heard many things, but I would like to know what

YOU think

I would like to know how you plan to implement

your revolution

How you plan to extricate it from its, no doubt,
provincial nature

Indeed, I would like to read anything you have a mind
to send me

Something other than dreams

Something other than mere talk

Something

—Letter sent from Nathan to Walter, 1978

* * *

A few weeks after the marathon, Richard cornered me in the apartment and demanded that we have a complete, in-person meeting of the NRF. He wanted to sit down with Walter and Paul and Alex, to regroup and reaffirm our commitment in person.

It was a test I was determined to pass. I contacted the others.

Walter was clearly not excited about the plan. He was still paranoid, saying that he heard my mother's private detective had recently started calling James again. James believed his house was watched; his phone possibly tapped. I wondered if Walter had told James anything about the conspiracy and the NRF. If he did, I knew he would deny he did. Still, he and James were friends. It was probably hard for him to keep such secrets from James, as it was for me not to include James in our conspiracy because of his past betrayal for returning to Michigan and abandoning our journey to the East, that now seemed so long ago.

These concerns it turned out, were mostly untrue. My family had engaged George Randolph again over the summer, when he approached them and offered to work pro bono. His reasons why have been lost to history and failing memories. Was he envisioning media attention when he cracked the case? Had my mother's grief, and the long and heart-wrenching letters she mailed him, touched his weathered heart? There's no way to know. But there are limited hours available for free investigations, and there's no evidence that Randolph, or anyone else, paid as much attention to James as they should have.

The more Walter made excuses, the more I was convinced we needed a meeting. The success of the NRF, as I envisioned it, was based on the personalities and genius of each member, more than on any specific policy or goal. This was a collaborative conspiracy. My idealism wouldn't allow me to seek a future for myself as a king, but with the power of the alpha minds combined, I was convinced our community of revolutionaries could upend systems entrenched for centuries. Words and tactics could be modified to adapt to changing circumstances, as I'd learned while writing *The NonLinguistics of History*, but the unique minds and creativity of the people making the changes could not be replaced. We needed brilliant minds prepared to adapt to events which could never be predicted. Only individual power, along with chance and serendipity, could make the impossible a reality.

We knew the impossible, but I needed each of these geniuses to make reality.

In late November 1978, Richard and I drove south around the southern tip of Lake Michigan, and then north to Holland. Paul was already on his way by train from the East Coast, where he'd enrolled in Princeton Seminary. Walter was driving separately from Chicago, where he worked for his father's finance company. Alex would arrive from Detroit. It was odd to think that none of us lived in or near Holland anymore, and yet when I'd proposed the meeting, no one questioned that it should happen there, in the shadow of the lake where Steven Kubacki disappeared.

There is poetry and truth in returning to the scene of the crime.

Snow was already piling up in drifts along the roadside when we arrived at Frank McAdam's house. He was out of town for a couple of weeks, according to Walter. Visiting family? Going on vacation with a new undergraduate friend? I don't think anyone asked. We simply took the opportunity fate had granted us.

Richard and I arrived first and picked the lock to Frank's back door to gain entry. We were burglars, criminals, trespassers now, all adding to our sense of grand adventure and righteous purpose.

By the time a fire was crackling in the fireplace, the others had arrived, and there was a different kind of crackling in the air. I instantly sensed the polarization among us. Though I hadn't seen my fellow conspirators for eight months, the only one to hug me was Paul. Like Richard, he'd clearly grown more fervent in his dedication to the NRF, but Walter and Alex seemed to be cooling. Walter barely looked at me. Alex busied himself in another room.

Still, I felt exhilaration in the moment of reuniting, and I relished the sense of connection among comrades as we sat in the weathered room, lit only by the fire. We offered updates—the Right Arm made progress in its quest to take over the three heads of the dragon, though the going was slow. Paul was in a prestigious seminary, Walter worked in international banking, and Richard affirmed his intent to go to law school after he finished his MFA. Alex, we all agreed, would find a way to influence and change the emerging area of high technology, which we agreed had potential that was not yet being used for or against the people.

There were few questions about the Left Arm, and the silence held daggers that pricked my conscience and skin. They knew already how little Nathan Stanfield had truly done.

We all affirmed they would keep working, no matter how long it took.

The snow fell in sticky clumps, coating the frozen shoreline of Lake Michigan, looking like crushed sulfur in the yellow moon. Somewhere out there, under all of the ice and snow, Steven Kubacki was still lost. Or was he? He was here, I knew, inside me, seeking another way.

What would happen, I wondered, if we all disappeared that night, and moved somewhere to start our own community—a brain trust to revolutionize the future? What if what we were called to wasn't revolution after all? But as I studied the beloved faces surrounding me, I already knew that was no longer a possibility. Steven's death had made sure of that, bound us by a conspiracy that weakened all other ties. Such a community would never happen. Good intentions were not enough.

Richard sensed my questions in the air, weaving around the hesitations of others. I watched as he grew worried at the wavering energy. He left the room and returned with a box that I recognized as Frank's prized coin collection. We would take this and sell it, he announced, to fund the NRF.

A new conspiracy, a new crime, a new set of secrets to bind us together. We were thieves now.

I was not the only person in the room to cringe. Only later did I consider that Richard was the only one among us who had never met Frank, didn't see him as an individual. Compassion over empathy was an easier choice when the one demanding empathy is a caricature, a missing presence, not real.

Still, no one in the house objected, and Walter put Frank's box in our car when we left.

On the drive home the next day, he talked excitedly and incessantly, already seeing himself as critical to the NRF's budding web of conspiratorial power brokering.

I sat quietly in the passenger seat, longing to get back to Natalie.

Finally, to distract us both, I turned on the dome light and read aloud from a book I'd "borrowed" from Frank's, *Beau Geste*. The richly told story followed the adventures of three English brothers who ran away from home to join the French Foreign Legion. As I read, Richard interrupted from time to time with odd comments about how the Foreign Legion still accepted almost anyone—even criminals and fugitives.

* * *

The winter arrived in earnest, cloaking Madison in snow and ice and creating a muted, strange interlude of quiet. The Dark Monk had fallen quiet. Richard's talk of revolution dulled, shifting to a contemplative quietness that was in some ways more unsettling. He was dating a pretty young woman named Amelia, and I assumed that was why he'd lost his zeal. If anyone knew the test of love at that point, I believed it was me.

I took advantage of Richard's distraction to spend more time seeking out Natalie. She wasn't always easy to find. She told me she didn't have a phone where she lived, and she often wasn't in the coffee shop. But when she was, her joy at seeing me filled me and felt genuine.

I told her one winter day that I was falling in love with her.

Her response was guarded. She didn't want to say anything about her feelings, she told me. She said instead she had terrible taste in men. She didn't trust herself.

Natalie had said things like this before. Her past remained cloaked in mystery, but I always wondered if there had been a marriage, a relationship she was fleeing; if that's why she kept everything so close, why she always seemed afraid of being known.

Her choice to keep me at arm's length didn't change how I felt about her. She knew me, felt me, cared for me, I was sure of that much. And her presence, despite her contradictions, meant that I wasn't alone.

That was a comfort and a conflict, because of course Nathan Stanfield was supposed to be alone. His very existence, the separation from Steven Kubacki, was based on the goal of being alone, untethered from any societal bindings or emotional connections. That was the only way for Nathan to do the ruthless things I was still convinced he needed to do. The only way to attract other loners capable of acting with total abandonment in service to our cause was to embrace aloneness.

Of course, it's obvious now what an enormous flaw in the NRF plans this was. There were plenty of reasons to doubt that I could find the extreme side of Nathan Stanfield, to embrace the power of the Dark Monk to become a cold-blooded killer. But now, with Natalie, I was discovering how impossibly hard it was for me—still carrying with me the affable, kind, loving Steven Kubacki—to even accept my role as a loner, or to sacrifice my desire for authentic relationships and connection to other people with whom I could explore existence.

Deep in my heart, hidden from everyone, I started to doubt that our revolution could succeed. That I could succeed. My mind whispered that I would be alone forever, that without intimate relationships, Nathan would lose his connections to higher dimensions, to other beings, to higher dimensional Stevens, and become terribly finite and worldly bound except for his connection to the Dark Monk and other darknesses that I preferred not to think of.

As I spiraled in my own thoughts and feelings, I hardly noticed that Richard disappeared for a few days. I assumed, if I thought at all, that he was at Amelia's, or maybe even that he was visiting his family in Atlanta. The holidays were close, a time for family and nostalgia for everyone except Nathan Stanfield.

I didn't question anything until one night when I went looking for the backpack where I kept all my writing—my personal journal, the NRF documents, my poetry—all of it jumbled together in notebooks and loose paper. I'd been to an art gallery with Natalie that night, and I wanted to write her a poem.

The notebook, though, was gone. Missing. Nowhere to be found.

It was all I could do not to panic. Where could it have gone? There was so much there to incriminate me, to incriminate all of us.

When Richard finally showed up again, several days later, I pounced as soon as he walked through the door. Had he taken the backpack to Amelia's? To his parents? Did he know what risk he'd put us in?

Richard smiled a coy, Cheshire cat smile. He had taken the backpack, he admitted. But it wasn't at Amelia's.

It was in France.

Richard's eyes were as cold as his smile. I'd been in Madison for too long, he said. I'd lost track of my mission, was doing nothing to advance the revolution. I put it at risk every day with the possibility of being found, of being caught alive. He had decided to do something to wake me up.

Richard's contemplative quietness hadn't been a loss of zeal after all, I realized. It had been a phase of planning. He had flown to France and, inspired by spy movies, left my backpack in a locker in a train station with what he called "a few other surprises." In another twist taken from spy movies, he claimed he could not remember which locker, nor even which station.

Was this a prank, an eviction? It was clearly a test of some kind.

I stood and walked out of our house in a daze. I was no longer in control.

* * *

The many choices of Nathan's and Steven's are small subplots in the much larger plots and purposes of higher dimensional systems. Those plots are beyond comprehension. We would like to believe they are primarily about us, but they are not. There are other more powerful forces/beings/energies that are in play, that the Steven of Light and the Steven of Darkness are unaware of. Decisions are not just Steven's or Nathan's. They are the decisions of a community.

But let's get real. This otherworldly community is not so focused on our little planet and its destiny and the destiny of some of its creatures, called humans. The community forgets about us because we are often insignificant or irrelevant. There are bigger issues at play than me or us or the Earth, and so sometimes their influences, intentional or not, while seemingly benign and appropriate for the time and the context, can go awry. When we call, they often do not come.

—From the Nexalistic Revolutionary Front (NRF)
Documents by Nathan T. Stanfield (NTS)
a.k.a. Steven Kubacki, 1978

* * *

Dear Nathan,

. . . Clearly you have identified the pathological identity; he is audible in your screams . . . Notice the parasitic manifestation evident in "Empiricism" and orthodox Marxism. In radical politics, this bourgeois sclerosis is most commonly found in anarchism, or its more pathetic form, fascism . . . Yet, be mindful, the rhetoric of anarchy will supply us with anarchists whose pathology I have no care to nurse . . .

Static or not-static, what I mean is "they" (typical friends and lovers) don't know what you're talking about. In a sense you can't help "them," because you cannot have any rapport with "them" whatsoever. . . Either one explodes with a creative resonance, filling cathedrals with the assiduity of fortissimo, or one implodes, peering ever inward, droning to the tune of one's "less likeliness."

The time is now! As the Apostle John quotes, "I go to prepare a place for you." The propitious moment shall declare with the communion prose, "Come, for all things are now ready."

—Letter from Paul, 1978

* * *

I went to find Natalie, seeking solace and escape, and entered the coffee shop to find her in a heated argument of her own with her friend, the shop's owner. As soon as she saw me at the door, she stormed past and out into the winter sunshine, grabbing my hand and pulling me along with her.

Natalie was clearly in no mindset to help me with Richard, so I held my tongue. We walked into the night, wreathed in a heady silence. Somewhere along the way, we joined a party at one of the campus fraternities for a few minutes. Natalie disappeared and returned with a handful of pills. She pressed several into my hand. "Take these."

I did, without even questioning what they were. That is how much I loved Natalie.

Only later did I realize that she hadn't taken these pills herself.

temporary lobotomy

It left my mind vacant

the drug
against the grain
i could not sleep
nor could i act

simply hell
i saw forms
no objects
for three days

i ascended
and descended stairs
in eternity
like a programmed ghost

—From the Nexalistic Revolutionary Front (NRF)
Documents by Nathan T. Stanfield (NTS)
a.k.a. Steven Kubacki, 1978

The drug, it turned out, was Haldol, a powerful antipsychotic prescription drug that's primarily used today to treat schizophrenia, mania, and hallucinations. Within hours, it had taken over my neurotransmitters and sent me into one of the worst drug experiences of my life. My body stopped being my own. My body jerked unnaturally and without my control. My mouth moved without me speaking. Someone, or something, was pulling strings attached to my limbs—making me dance like a puppet, like that Christian I'd seen on my first acid trip.

I had never been so cut off from myself—so isolated within my own body, with no connection to the universe. It was severe disassociation, only on a negative scale I never thought possible. I was torn in two, manic and desperately falling asleep in every moment.

It was incredibly painful and utterly terrifying, and it lasted for three long days. Natalie disappeared. I may have abandoned her, or she may have abandoned me. Richard found me and brought me home. The alarm was clear on his face when he saw me, although I couldn't respond to it. Our previous conflict was forgotten. I remember that he took a softball and played catch with me, trying to bring my coordination back. At some point, we agreed that if I didn't get better, he'd drug me and throw me into a nearby river with heavy chains and weights. Steven Kubacki's body could not be found in Madison, Wisconsin.

Slowly, on the third day, the Haldol wore off, and my connection to the universe returned. When the dam finally and fully did burst, everything flooded back. I felt my body, the multiverse, the Dark Monk, my quantum selves—I felt the air itself in a different way.

I saw myself as I truly was. All I'd wanted my whole life was to be loved, to belong, to be part of a community of purpose and curiosity. Why not accept those pulls of belonging, be tempted to accept the world as it was, and end all this drama, seek personal fulfillment and love, and escape. But that was not remotely possible. The sufferings of my early years and the intoxicating quality of the multiverses I'd explored since would not allow it. The world still suffered; people suffered.

In a waking vision after my rebirth from Haldol, I saw myself on a ship sailing forward in turbulent seas, nearly capsizing. To save myself like Odysseus in the ancient Greek epic of the *Odyssey,* I tied myself to its mast. The sirens on the shore were calling me with irresistible voices to sail into rocky reefs. I knew in that rapturous state I could not refuse their call. I could not refuse the NRF or the Dark Monk.

When I emerged from that frightening vision, I fell into a different and more favorable one. It had the quality of an actual timeline that I believed could occur. I saw Nathan Stanfield addressing the United Nations, talking about a new economic approach to save humanity from planetary destruction. It was to be based on valuation systems other than money, but even as I listened, the words slipped from my mind. I couldn't recall them, couldn't understand them, or where they might have come from. There were ideas of radical transparency and accountability, with leadership based on meritocracy, not wealth, and world democracy.

I judged that as a sign, the universe's way of telling me what I had to do next. Richard was right. It was time for Nathan to move on.

Richard wasn't home when all of this happened, and so as soon as I felt like I had full control of my body again, I went looking for him. I started at Amelia's.

The hour was early, and she opened the door wearing only a towel, fresh from the shower. Richard was in class, she said, but she invited me in to wait.

If you can see where this is going, reader, you are more prescient than I was in the moment. I walked inside, sat on the couch, and waited while Amelia got dressed and made tea. We started to talk. Still born again from the depths of Haldol, I offered warmth and gratitude.

Amelia put her hand on my leg. I leaned in and kissed her. After months of Natalie's aloof physicality, this openness drew me. But even as I made my way to her bed, I knew this was a test that I was failing. I failed my friend and comrade, though to my knowledge, he never found out. Amelia and I were innocently sitting on the couch again when he came to her apartment a few hours later.

As I spoke to Richard, I jumped in with the revelation that had come from Haldol. The whole time I was trapped inside myself, I told him, I was thinking about the book we read on the way back from Holland—*Beau Geste* and the French Foreign Legion.

When we were away from Amelia's apartment and back at home, I laid out my complete plan: I would fully embrace the Left Arm by joining the French Foreign Legion.

* * *

November 27, 1978

Now I know what it is — not an "obsession" as told to me by my son, daughter, and husband, but love. Plain, simple love for my son — the one who is lost — that makes me need to find him — to offer my hand and comfort if possible and ask for another chance to let me love him and do better. I do so little actually — It is so pathetic — the small amounts of money I glean from my paycheck here and there to finance what — a few ads and one or two trips? And even this appears to be too much! For those who feel neglected — for those who feel my time, thoughts, and money would be better spent on what????? How stingy with time, thoughts, and even my money they are. Have they ever thought this through??? Who else will look for him, who else will ever think of him, who else will want him home, close, or at least to know that he is well, safe, and happy. Who??? He is important — as important as they are, and maybe even more so since he is the one who is lost. Why am I made to feel guilty, or is it my own guilt that I feel? I explain, and no one hears or understands my feelings for my son, [feelings I would have] even for them if they were to be the one who is missing. Even this does not explain — the only way anyone will ever understand is if it happens to them, and perhaps even then they will not.

—A note from Irene Pegg

Chapter 11

THE FRENCH FOREIGN LEGION

With dexterity we shall asunder the precepts of logic
Our chill will heat the earth
We are obliged to find a new culture
In nonlinguistics it shall be found
Premonitions of disaster that await the wicked
The answer is unaccountable
We meddle in the world of kings
And stir the people into temptation
For behold the morning before we were
There crying in the dark of weathered wane clouds
Cry no more
For the heroes are red streaming across the land
Waving undulating in revelation of you
Your feedback is sensual
Your unearthliness expounds wonder
Viscid in its colors

— From The NonLinguistics of History by Steven Kubacki, 1977

I never saw Amelia again.

Richard and I imbibed many shots of whisky with tears in our eyes that week, recommitting ourselves to our friendship and to the NRF.

And then I was on a bus from Wisconsin to New Jersey, the first leg in the journey to return Nathan T. Stanfield to his mission. My mind was still a little blurred and buzzed from the Haldol, and so I passed hours of open highways through Midwestern farm fields feeling like a television tuned to heavy static. I tried to think about Natalie, about my family, about my mission, but could summon no response or emotion.

Was this compassionate ruthlessness at last? My mind filled with hope and welcomed the relief from regrets, from guilt. I embraced my future in the French Foreign Legion, notorious home of men hiding from disgrace, crime, or other dark places—and yet the safest place I could be.

By the time the bus reached Pennsylvania, I was filled with a giddy certainty that the Legion would train me to become a soldier, that I would lead the NRF to a glorious future, and that the Earth would then be free of poverty and war, and deserts would become fields of produce and grain.

This exhilaration lasted for hours before the Haldol struck me down again, my grandiosity shattering like a cheap mirror that reflected only a man struck down by his own mortality and fragility. The possibility of death existed not only in the multiverse where I lived with Natalie, but in my present path of danger.

My emotions were still swinging wildly when I got off the bus in Princeton, New Jersey, and walked a block into the winter night to find Paul waiting for me in his car. We were on a clandestine mission and did not want to be seen together. Not yet.

I spent long, glorious days in Paul's apartment, staying out of sight during daylight, slinking into out-of-the-way bars late at night. Strangely, I felt no urgency to leave, though the calling of the Foreign Legion could not be silenced and NRF documents in a locker in Paris were threatened with imminent discovery. The holidays flowed past and around me; my first Christmas as Nathan Stanfield—my first year without my family, without donning a Santa Claus suit for the amusement of my extended relations, especially my young cousins. A large part of me missed that simple togetherness and effortless good cheer.

Paul sensed my shifting moods, and unlike Richard, met me with pastoral understanding, inspiration, and encouragement. At his urging, we talked late into the night about theology, revolution, and the clarity of the insane. Paul regarded me as a man of impeccable praxis, he said, using the Greek word for action. He told me that I was a dialectical prophet of sorts, vulnerable and open in my flaws and charmingly irresistible for those willing to see. I was a man set apart, chosen, my body woven with threads made by alien hands. He, perhaps more than any, understood I was in some way more than human, intimate yet elsewhere.

Paul saw me as a martyr, a position intrinsic and venerated in his religious worldview, self-sacrificing for the common good. He believed in redemption, in never giving up on me despite my repeated missteps and failures. I could be forceful in my arguments, but Paul saw that I could also be humbled, even if I resisted such humbling.

I lingered in Princeton longer than I intended, finally feeling seen without having to prove myself. After Richard's fiery judgment and Natalie's apathy, Paul's steady inspiration was a balm.

In many ways, my presence was a gift for Paul as well. His visions and openness to the future, to the multiverse, to the powers beyond his understanding, expanded. I could see that he was struggling with his own loneliness, having carried halfway across the country a secret that couldn't be shared with any of his classmates or friends. The more we talked, the more his spark ignited. He even suggested at one point that he quit seminary and join the Foreign Legion with me. He would fulfill his call to the NRF, he said, not through years of study and advancing through church politics, but by pressing God's call for a Christian crusade made earthly.

The thought of a travel and training companion drew me, but I knew it could never be. Without Paul firmly embedded in the Church, the Right Arm would lose a crucial component of its moral authority. Better he stayed behind and kept his hands clean. Of all of the NRF members, Paul was the one whose skills and attitudes were the most irreplaceable in my mind. There could be other financiers, other politicians, if called on. But Paul's particular approach to traditional religion was unlike any I'd heard before.

I'd never met anyone who understood spirituality in conjunction with modern science, especially in terms of quantum mechanics and other dimensions and realities. No one who both subscribed to religious faith and saw that God and Jesus were inherent in all things. From the beginning, Paul had led the discussion of how to bring the ancient dragon's head of Religion into line with NRF by adapting Christianity to fit our goals. He believed that to become an effective shepherd of Christianity, he would need to be circumspect about what to reveal for people to open their hearts to God's will. For most people, that meant gently pushing them beyond their comfort zone to embrace new spiritual interpretations, while at the same time comforting and supporting them in their doubts. The details of theology were malleable and shifted as times changed throughout history. What Paul planned to tell the resistant about God's word would be essentially the same as what he told those ready to embrace a revolutionary doctrine. However, how that was articulated and ritualized through the guidance of Jesus might be a little different, so that the seeds of God's word could take root. Paul was regularly delivering sermons to congregations in several churches and felt that many would harken, including some ministers he knew.

He ardently believed that the NRF was chosen by God to make the world a better place—a more Christian place of love, freedom, and democracy. And while I had my doubts about his deity, I ardently believed in Paul's ability to make it happen.

I told him to wait, to stay in seminary. I would check out the Foreign Legion alone and let him know if it was worth it.

* * *

I have placed all hope
in the ambiguity of hexagrams*
the Future wherein all hope lies
I have learned to avoid
determinations of the past
that I might remain its unknowing lackey
I have compelled the present
to act frantic (whether in a stab of passivity or panic)
so that I accomplish nothing
I have practiced daydreaming
as a profession

so that I can believe I think
I have developed the art of writing
so that absorbed action
can pretend significance

Lastly,
I have assumed leadership (an arcane knowledge of sorts)
when all the while
I was just loud-mouthed and desperate

*Hexagrams are the configurations used in the I-Ching to provide wisdom and to understand potential futures.

—From the Nexalistic Revolutionary Front (NRF)
Documents by Nathan T. Stanfield (NTS)
a.k.a. Steven Kubacki, 1978

* * *

Shortly after Christmas, Paul and I pooled our money and bought me a cheap one-way ticket to London. For some reason that was much cheaper than flying to Paris, but I reasoned that I could cross into France by boat, hitchhike to Paris to retrieve my writings, and then head to Calais, where I'd heard that the recruitment office for the Foreign Legion was located.

It was quite a plan, perhaps the most forward-thinking of our revolution to date.

Which meant, of course, that it would be tested.

Two nights before my flight, we heard a knock on Paul's door. I remember the two of us froze. My first irrational thought was that my mother's private investigator had tracked me down, or maybe even the police.

The truth was even more unexpected.

We found Natalie standing there, soaking wet, shivering as if she'd run the entire way from Madison to Princeton. To this day, I still don't know how she found me there; through Richard, perhaps, but she was resourceful.

I pulled her inside, wrapping both arms around her waist and pressing my cheek to her wet cheek.

I turned and introduced her to Paul. "Here is Natalie, the woman who can turn me aside."

"Are you an angel?" Paul asked with a mischievous smile.

"Are you my Nathan's Mephistopheles?" she quipped back.

"I would say it's probably the other way around," he laughed.

Not knowing what else to do, I offered Natalie a bowl of stew and a loaf of bread that Paul had made.

"I need to do some reading at the seminary," he announced. "Maybe I'll see you both later?" Paul sensed the magical energy between us and told me later he worried if that energy was enough to alter my plans.

When Natalie was done eating and warmed up, she and I took a walk, and soon found ourselves hitchhiking down a busy highway, hand in hand. She said something about going to Vermont, but we made it as far as northern New Jersey, somewhere near a lake. We broke into a large, empty summer home with ease and started a fire in the fireplace. I told her about my plan to join the Legion. And then I did something I'd never done before. I told her my name—my *real* name.

It was an incredibly important moment for me, but Natalie barely responded. I could tell there was something bothering her, that she was hiding a big secret of her own.

There was a long pause, and then the question I did not expect. She told me that she'd left Madison and was moving to Vermont. She asked me to give up the revolution and come back to the world of the living. She said if I did, she would finally love me the way I loved her. She threw her arms around me, pulling me tightly, and we kissed for a long time.

I was tempted, so tempted. How badly I wanted to end it all and throw myself into her arms. But I had already failed one recent test from the universe. I wasn't going to make that mistake twice.

And so, I told her no.

I chose the NRF. I left Natalie at the lake house that night. There was something about her that wasn't reliable. I went back to Princeton, and two days later, I boarded a plane for London.

* * *

The sun does not rise
without first
thinking of you
The stars don't appear
without seeing
you are the reason they shine
The Earth groans
when you are not there to bless it
The winds are calling

I am calling

The days are shortening

My hands are trembling

The universe is ending

Why are you taking

your love away?

—Early poetry by Steven Kubacki

I am the front line

I accept the impossible

I actualize world madness

I am every man's secret

The vision

The power

The revolution in

consciousness that smashes

the zeitgeist

the conformity

the all-pervasive banality

I rise above the idiot and genius

stepping on their mystery

like manure

—From the Nexalistic Revolutionary Front (NRF) Documents by Nathan T. Stanfield (NTS) a.k.a. Steven Kubacki, 1978

* * *

I crossed the Atlantic, feeling like Jonah in the belly of the whale. Though resolute in my interpretation of the universe's plan, I nonetheless stewed over Natalie's invitation. Had I made a terrible mistake in refusing her?

My mind shifted, dissociated. Timelines and alternative histories competed with each other. I saw myself milking cows in Vermont with two older children jumping in the hay. There was a ring on my finger, and I knew Natalie had one too. But it didn't last. Later, I saw myself as an older man in an ice crevasse struggling with a broken leg and arm, the light many meters above fading into darkness. I guess it was good while it lasted, I mused—a timeline that a love-addled mind might choose.

I had passed the cosmic test. Duty triumphed. The Dark Monk won, showing me that there were other timelines bigger than my own, with purposes I did not and could not know but could not help. I saw many alternative histories—Walter was in some of them, but so was the waitress at the bar, my higher goatee self, and extradimensional beings, all competing to determine whose cosmic song would co-opt or control the others or aspects of others.

It was egocentric to think my choice of timeline was mine alone. I had committed the human-centric fallacy, believing my universe to be the center or the only one, with individual humans in central control of their destinies, and so on. The multiverse was an indifferent totality, complex beyond comprehension, and perhaps uncaring of human aspirations, attributions, and interpretations. Sometimes what was right in one moment was wrong in the next or never took place at all.

Consumed by such daunting thoughts, I landed at London Heathrow in a dissociative daze. I once again cleared passport control using Steven Kubacki's passport without issue and reached the city by sundown.

Hours passed, but I could not say for certain what I did to fill the time. I have vague recollections of sitting beneath the statue of Boadicea in her chariot and throwing stones into the filthy Thames. The omnipresent hum of the city seemed distant, hive-like and removed.

Only when a pretty university student, Wendy, approached me in a pub later that night did my mind snap back to the present. We exchanged small talk, though it hardly seemed necessary. After a few lifeless, warm beers, she invited me to stay with her at her aunt's flat. There, on a comfy couch in the center of the cold, damp living room, we talked in the light of a small fireplace. I wondered if I'd entered a Dickens novel.

Wendy studied astrophysics and believed that space exploration and colonization could save humanity from the inevitable—an uninhabitable planet due to overpopulation and environmental destruction. I agreed with her wholeheartedly, but when our conversation ranged into politics and economics, we found themselves on different footing. Wendy believed all attempts to improve spaceship Earth were futile, that only off-planet could anything really change. The history of humans could not be reversed, she claimed. I countered with the ideals of the NRF, without naming it, and said that a revolution on Earth would make possible the colonizing of the moon or Mars. Technology and science were not sufficient for revolution, I said, but needed radical political and economic guidance. In my mind, though, I wondered if perhaps Wendy was right. If so, the NRF was nothing more than Don Quixote battling windmills.

Having reached an impasse, we did what young people do and went to bed. I was transported by our nonverbal communion, the energetic union of two old souls. There are quantum entanglements between people that transcend time and universes, and I had found one.

A lightness of being I need
To offset the heavy responsibilities
Of saving the world
From destruction

A pretty girl
Whose eyes I can fall in
Like an abyss of starlight
With legs of refuge
For touch-starved hands

I want to dance
In the trance of her tasseled hair
Superficial
Until I die.

—From the Nexalistic Revolutionary Front (NRF)
Documents by Nathan T. Stanfield (NTS)
a.k.a. Steven Kubacki, 1978

The next morning, I rose before the sun and escaped the apartment without waking Wendy. In the predawn chill, I made my way to St. Pancras railway station and booked passage to Paris via a combination of train and ferry. I don't remember much about the trip itself. There were rocky seas crossing the Channel. I was very detached and alone.

* * *

My first priority was to find the backpack. I had no idea where Richard had stashed it, but my train took me to Gare du Nord, which seemed like a good place to start.

I passed through the lofty building and made my way to the office where lost and found luggage was kept. Railway officials, I'd learned in earlier travels, emptied storage lockers periodically, and many weeks had passed since Richard's unexpected trip abroad. My things had certainly been moved, touched. I didn't worry much about it. Would French rail workers stop to read notebooks full of scribbled English ideas?

Obviously, I had no key or ticket to prove that I owned anything. In broken French I explained my situation to the clerk behind the counter—a friend had accidentally left my red frame backpack in a locker when he returned to the United States. I had just arrived from the USA and wished to reclaim it.

Somehow the station agents not only understood me but believed me. They took me to a back room full of items jumbled together in bins and even helped me dig through the piles. Minutes stretched as we grunted and stretched, but at last one of the agents shouted for me to come over. He had pulled a familiar red backpack out from under a pile of luggage and held it up. As he hefted it, I saw a strain, then a look of confusion came over his face. The pack had a funny shape—something in it was heavy, long and protruding. Richard had left me more than just my notebooks.

I chuckled and tried to look like everything was as I expected it. The agent gave me the backpack without too much trouble, and I got the hell out of there before anyone thought to ask me more questions. What had Richard put in there? I didn't open the bag until I reached a park—probably Parc Monceau. The day was cold, but French families were all around me, enjoying the weak winter sunbreak before another round of rain sent us all ducking back to shelter.

I pulled out my notebooks first, assuring myself that they were all just as Richard said. Underneath the paper, my hand touched cold metal. Without thinking about the people watching, I pulled out a collapsible rifle and a pistol.

I remembered the park, the families, the strict gun laws of Europe, and I shoved them all back into the pack.

How did Richard get guns like this? Did he buy them on the French black market? Smuggle them from the States? I never had the chance to ask. I'll never know.

What was clear was that he'd left the guns to me, with me, in the possession of the Left Arm. It was a challenge, a dare, a reminder of what I was called to do.

It terrified me.

When the rain inevitably started again, I made my way to a mostly deserted Moroccan café nearby. I ordered tea to give myself time to think. One cup turned into three or four, then a meal. Before I noticed the time, it was dark outside, and I had nowhere to stay and almost no money. I had learned earlier that the Foreign Legion did not recruit in Calais but in Aubagne. Buying a train ticket to Aubagne, the city in the south of France where the Foreign Legion did their selection and incorporation, would take more of my travel funds than I expected.

The owner of the café, a kindly old Moroccan man, talked to me a few times. He could tell I was in some kind of trouble and said for just a few francs I could stay at his apartment upstairs.

The apartment was small, but it smelled amazing, and the walls were painted an unsettling shade of red. The café owner's wife had passed away some months ago, he said. Here was another man, lonely and pursuing a goal alone.

As we ate dinner together, I told him I had come to France to join the Legion. He frowned. I told him about the stolen backpack that had left the United States with notebooks and ideas but had been full of guns when I rediscovered it in Paris. He shook his head as if to say that I was making a mistake.

Still, the next morning, I asked the Moroccan man if I could leave the guns with him, promising to come back for them later. His eyes were sad as he studied me, but he nodded, and then he showed me a hiding place in the back of his closet, behind a wall panel. He gave me 500 francs for traveling money. I never saw him again.

I think he knew I was never coming back.

* * *

Nate,

You are, of course, alive while S is dead . . . WS begins his financial rise to power. He accepts his degradation for the sake of Nathan. You will be hungry, tired, wounded, oppressed, but will rise from the desert. You must. It is my reason for being alive. It is my fear . . .

Now it is time for you to forget us and shut up and go; risk, survive, and arise to save the right from oblivion. Fuck you, you God damned egotistical emotionalist. Where are all your great doctrines now. Get out, Get out, Begin, Begin, Your followers, your armies, our destiny, or else, We Are Doomed.

—Letter from Walter Smith to Nathan T. Stanfield, 1978

Returning to Gare du Nord, I used some of my newly acquired money to upgrade my train ride to Aubagne in southern France. Seated in a fancy car with businessmen and socialites, I pored over my reclaimed writings in the hope that they held more hidden signs from the universe. Outside, the countryside seemed to be the same blur I had traveled past the day before. The train went south. Finally, the city came into view like a premonition, though charming like most towns in the limestone hills of southern France. For me, however, the long and uneventful trip had the concurrent vision of traveling through the land of Mordor to the fortress of Barad-dûr in Tolkien's *Lord of the Rings*. My unease spiked.

Aubagne was a commune with communist mayors about a thousand feet above sea level and was politically and socially entirely the opposite to what I would be joining. After walking and getting lost, I was surprised to see a line of men stretching down the sidewalk and up to the door of the French Foreign Legion. It hadn't occurred to me that there would be so many other recruits. A flicker crossed my mind—what if they don't want me—but I pushed it aside.

Just then, the door to the building opened, and a Legion officer in an olive uniform and with the whitest hat I'd ever seen waved everyone inside. The staff, it seemed, was just getting back from lunch.

I glanced at the officer as I passed him going in the door, and another flicker crossed my mind—a warning. The man before me stared straight ahead, with no expression. No inner light. He was a lightbulb without electricity. Someone had flipped the switch, pulled the plug long ago.

And yet the universe had brought me this far. I would not falter or fail again. I walked past him and added the name Nathan T. Stanfield to the list of new recruits to the French Foreign Legion.

First, we had to give up all our clothes and don legionnaire clothing. After a brief but thorough physical and medical examination along with lots of running, pushups, and pullups, I filled out piles of paperwork and intake forms, some of which seemed to be psychological tests. One of the unique aspects of the Legion, at least in 1979, was that recruits could enlist under whatever name they chose—a *nom de guerre*—and even name a nationality other than their own. No one seemed to check passports or verify identity, which was an added inducement to those desperate souls, like Nathan T. Stanfield, who wanted a way to disappear. Anyway, I had stashed my passport and other belongings in a locker at the train station in case things did not go according to plan, as they often had not in the past. Almost none of the other candidates spoke English, so I kept mainly to myself in the mess hall and my bunk bed, which was worse than any hostel's.

Once I passed the initial screening, I was then interrogated by a Norwegian corporal who spoke good English. He wanted to know why I was there. I said I wanted adventure, travel, and to forget about a failed relationship. He asked about drugs, criminal records, and anything he could think of to intimidate me. His voice boomed and often accused me of lying. I kept to my script. However, he searched me and found my student ID in a jacket pocket I had forgotten about. That seemed to satisfy him that I wasn't a criminal and had an identity. For being a student, he ridiculed me. He didn't care what name I went by now. Once I officially contracted and joined the Legion, which would be required of me after some initial training to determine if I had what it took, he would be my new teacher—a different kind of teacher. He laughed.

After several days of cleaning latrines, doing pushups, running incessantly in place, and being harassed as often as possible, I was instructed to climb aboard a sleek bus with the other recruits of the day who had been directed for initial training. A uniformed Legion soldier I had not yet met, this one wearing sunglasses to hide his eyes, drove us across town without a word of explanation.

I glanced around, considering my cohort. It was a much smaller group than those who had lined up at the door. The Legion was particular and skilled at weeding out those who were not prepared, physically or mentally, for the brutality of the legionnaire's life, that is, before they signed a three-year contract.

Most of the men on the bus seemed older than me, more worn by life and experience. Faces and knuckles were webbed with faded scars. I'd seen enough to know that they came from around the world, though I was the only recruit who claimed America as home. Few, I was relieved to see, spoke French. However, English was not their default language—grunting, grimacing, and pointing were. I had to learn some French if I were to survive. That was made a little easier with all the recruits singing Legionnaire songs together, almost all of which I did not understand.

During several hours on the bus, I saw many touristy towns with cathedrals, ancient Roman aqueducts, vineyards, and fortified castles. Suddenly, the bus pulled up to a compound. It was fenced in unadorned iron, behind which I could see a fortress-like building. I had seen this place before, in my visions.

In the town of Castelnaudary, the compound seemed like a farm, but it was really a military base. It was secretly guarded by men with high caliber machine guns and staffed with officers who shouted at lines of other recruits standing at attention in the courtyard. I remembered the Japanese dojo, and I could see the version of myself that had stayed, had maintained the routine of discipline there, among ranks of monks in training. This reality was a hundred times more violent. These men were going to order me to do more than beg for change in the park.

They were soldiers, mercenaries, and contract killers.

And so was I. Nathan T. Stanfield was going to become a soldier. My mind detached from considering any of the consequences.

Over the next several days, my group of recruits would see most areas of the Legion's compound as we experienced the French equivalent of early basic training. First were the tests to determine motivation, psychological preparedness, and probably much more that I wasn't even aware of. Then there was the physical conditioning. From sunup to sundown, legionnaires shouted at us in rapid French and raced us through cavernous gymnasiums where pitiless men taught some beginning hand-to-hand fighting techniques. For those who had weathered the first few weeks already and were official legionnaires, there would be training in weaponry.

We were bused here and there and marched and ran for miles with rifles without bullets (the MAS 49/56; very outdated by today's standards). We maintained a good distance from the target range, where gunfire rolled like thunder and cordite turned the air sulfurous. There were serpentine tunnels that fed into bunkers and underground caches. We ate colorless gruel—chicken, rice, bread, something green at dinner—in silence for at least two meals a day, accompanied by a single glass of stale red wine. We were being broken, reformed into an elite group devoid of ego or individualism. And everywhere, there were men with expressionless faces, devoid of inner light.

I did not keep my journal or write anything down during this time. I had left all that back in a locker in Aubagne. I didn't want to know what would happen if men like this found them and discovered what I was planning for the future.

* * *

Devoid of insistence
We swiftly slice through existence
It's warm butter reality.

For the past is like a vociferous cow
that had its tongue cut out
but still bellows

So let us not be cows
The unreasonable must be studied
Unreasonable methods embraced
unreasonable words sprinkled like star dust
Unreasonable motives gnawed to the bone

—From The Nonlinguistics of History
by Steven Kubacki, 1977

I had been an unsigned trainee for a little more than a week when it all came crashing down. In the darkest hours of the night, our barracks door slammed open and the lights all came on. I sat up in my bunk to see what was causing the commotion and recognized a few of the prefects. They dragged a body, slumped and unresisting, between them.

They shouted in French, angry, waving their arms for all of the recruits to come and watch what they would do. My mind warned me not to go, to stay in bed and shut out the violence. But Nathan could not say no. Nathan went and watched.

The prefects, as far as I could understand, had tracked down and caught a recruit who had deserted the Legion several weeks before my arrival. They'd brought him here as a warning, an open display of what awaited anyone who tried to abandon their pledge to France.

They'd clearly already beaten the man, who was bleeding so much from the face that I couldn't see his features. He may have been Turkish. They continued to beat him in front of us all.

And then they threw him into the center of the room and ordered all of us, the newest recruits, to join in. Many of the soldiers seemed happy to comply. As they pounced, I held back, watching as if in a trance. I saw the moment that the deserter's jaw broke.

After a few long minutes, or maybe just seconds, the prefects called off the recruits and dragged the deserter back out into the night. I couldn't tell if the man was dead or alive.

The lights were turned off, the men settled onto their bunks all around me.

This wasn't a game anymore. This wasn't just physical and mental conditioning.

The Dark Monk, dormant since I left Madison, stirred to life once more, activating powerful channels in my mind opened by the trauma I'd just witnessed.

I am a legionnaire somewhere in Africa. I can feel the oppressive heat of the sun, like I've never felt before or since. I point a machine gun at a group of prisoners, and I know that they are starving diamond miners. I feel an impulse, and before I realize what it is, I have squeezed the trigger and killed them all.

I see myself parachuting onto the top of a snowy mountain range and skiing down a steep bowl with a knapsack and rifle over my shoulder. As I near a building, perhaps a temple, I stop and fire a rocket. The building explodes even as people—families, children—try to exit.

Next, in the night I cross a river in a jungle, my gun raised above my head. The soldier in front of me suddenly disappears, and I hear someone hiss, "Crocodiles!"

I see myself in a brown monk's robe next. I think many years have passed, and I am out of the Legion, leading the Left Arm from Mexico City. I am watching news reports about a train station bombing, and know it was our work, the work of the NRF, using a man with terminal brain cancer as a suicide bomber. The loss of life is staggering, but I feel nothing. I know there are many terminal patients blowing themselves up around the world at that very moment. The revolution is worldwide. The NRF is known across South America, Africa, Europe, and the southeastern United States. If I go outside, I will see graffiti on building walls, on street after street, with the initials NRF in black and red, and the figure of a monk with a hood drawn up over his face.

The visions accelerate, with flashes of the future. People stand in long lines, reminiscent of bread lines. I see banks blown up and robbed and the money given to needy people. NRF activists fill the prisons, but many more are never caught, because we are aided by sympathizers in the police and FBI.

I see the Right Arm. I see Richard as president, elected to restore law and order and end the depression. I hear him speak to a joint session of Congress about how America will defeat the NRF and never bend to its radical ideas. Later, near the end of his term, he meets me secretly at some facility in the mountains. He is so happy to see me, and we talk about how our plans are nearing fruition. Walter is also there. He has financed Richard's political machine and funneled money into the NRF. We agree the NRF should both unleash more violence and at the same time strengthen its shadow economy, based on values like the communalism of the early Christians, advocated by the Church under Paul's direction.

Richard leaves, and the next time I see him it is on TV as he declares martial law. The Left and the Right Arm battle. I can see smoke and fires in cities, and then the planned surrender of the Left. NRF members are given amnesty by Richard's government, avoiding an expanding civil war, and many integrate into the US military. Walter's corporate and financial empire and Paul's new Christian church support the president on this union. The Constitution is amended to democratize all businesses and end all authoritarianism.

We had done it.

Or had we?

Now I see the suicide bombings of major corporate headquarters, the assassinations of executives. I see members of the US military, now infiltrated and one with the NRF. They assassinate Richard. And then, to my own horror, I see myself shoot Walter in the head.

I know that Walter gave me the gun to do it. He was complicit in his own death, and he couldn't handle it anymore; his wealth transferred to the NRF. But still, I have killed my best friend.

As the country burns, I step out of the shadows and reveal myself as the hooded monk of the NRF. Together, Paul and I declare a union of the New Christian Church with a true democratic America. Peace is established and I see colonies on the moon. The prophecy of the NRF has been fulfilled.

But still, I have killed my best friend.

The visions press into me. It is as if I'd taken acid, as if I was tripping right there in the barracks. Violence is the drug this time, and it is more powerful than anything I'd experienced before. The Dark Monk, the dark presence of my childhood, all of my most violent impulses from across the multiverse—they have all come alive.

The visions fade at last, and I feel myself being pulled out of the barracks, out of the Legion, out of France.

I sit up, sweating, and look around at the men snoring around me. Killers, all of them. Their faces grow dimmer by the day. I've watched them pile on to beat the deserter. And suddenly, finally, completely, I understand that my path would make me just like them. I could become what these men are—ruthless and violent sociopaths, without conscience or empathy. Not only could I do it, but I would have to, in order to make the vision of the NRF come true. Revolution seems not possible without violence.

Without me, without the Left Arm, the revolution will fail.

Yet am I willing to accept the consequences of what would emerge?

Part of me says yes. The otherness that has followed me all my life—the alienation, the inner turmoil—has stockpiled more rage than I can ever comprehend. That part can embrace villainy—will even seek it.

But the rest of me—those parts that still long for and seek love and a way to connect in compassion with the universe—will not, cannot accept it. For the first time, I clearly perceive my own humanity and how I must not sacrifice it.

The means do not justify the ends, even if the ends are a radically new world.

I have to get out.

The next morning, I run.

* * *

If Nathan felt me, which I know he did — after all, we were the same person (or were we) — it would have seemed like I was from a nether-verse. I do not mean a netherworld, which is generally depicted as a kind of hell, but rather a universe that is so otherworldly that it defies all linear explanations.

Clouds can manifest themselves in all kinds of formations — perpetually changing, growing, dissipating. What if that was the form of communication that came from the nether-verse? We humans would be hard pressed to make sense of it, though we might feel its truth and appreciate its wonder.

—From the Nexalistic Revolutionary Front (NRF)
Documents by Nathan T. Stanfield (NTS)
a.k.a. Steven Kubacki, 1979

Chapter 12
THE END OF THE NRF

Illumination. . . Our situation in Europe is hopeless. It does not further to continue a charade of possibilities when those possibilities do not exist. . . Why I ever agreed to this nonsense in the first place is a wonder. It was symptomatic of our failures and potential disasters — wishful thinking — the need of a plan to action which appeared the easiest. Other means to substantiation were never considered. Personally, I cannot handle another Japan debacle. The French Foreign Legion was a program chosen because of its meager costs (hence quickly sanctioned) and because its definitive structure offered security (a place to be) and NO imagination. . . The FFL is notorious, and its legionnaires are branded. Affiliation precludes any chance of cooperation with radicals and radical organizations in and outside the US Enlistment irrevocably mars the future; consequently, association to it is limited to fascists, thugs, and psychopaths. During the years I would have squandered in the FFL, a firm base of operations and an evolving network of contacts and those sympathetic to our cause could have been established in the United States and elsewhere. . .

—From the Nexalistic Revolutionary Front (NRF)
Documents by Nathan T. Stanfield (NTS)
a.k.a. Steven Kubacki, 1979

Unrelenting rains whipped the empty, predawn streets as I made my escape. Behind me, the Legion's fortress cast a psychological shadow that pursued me no matter which way I twisted and turned. I still heard the prefects' fists and boots striking the Turkish deserter. That drowned out the pressure of the Dark Monk, who wanted nothing more than to return to the Legion before anyone noticed and make manifest a future of violence.

Leaving my legionnaire clothes behind, I made my way to the nearest train station and slipped onto the first train bound for Aubagne, there picked up my passport and backpack from a locker, and then headed out to Paris. Though I had paid for my tickets, I often hid in the lavatory, afraid someone would catch me. I had changed into the street clothes I'd arrived in. Still, I was worried someone would pick me out as a deserter. I'd never signed the contract to officially become a legally-bound legionnaire, but I was afraid that wouldn't matter.

Confined to that tiny space, with the train swaying back and forth, I faced the Dark Monk. I built light traps in my mind to contain his attacks, the technique I have mentioned before to hold other dark presences at bay, but my hold on him was tenuous. From Paris, I took the train to Strasbourg, but did not visit James's mother in Belgium, recalling how she had cleverly divided us and how James had betrayed our mission.

In Strasbourg, I hopped off the French train and found another, bound for the last place where I could feel sort of myself and sort of more in control: Freiburg.

The NRF was dead. The Left Arm had failed. Nothing the Dark Monk said or did could change my mind.

I was done letting the universe point me in a direction and blindly following it. The universe guided me so well in the past. After teetering close to the edge of a dark abyss, barely recovering and pulling back before I toppled in, I needed to connect with a version of Steven Kubacki who existed before the NRF—before Nathan Stanfield. And the closest, strongest ties to my true past life—not a parallel one from a weird dimension, but part of who I'd been in this world—occurred in Freiburg.

Of course, Steven Kubacki was dead, a fact I conveniently forgot until Astrid saw me standing on her doorstep and screamed. She sprang back into her house. I imagined she thought I was a ghost or zombie. She fled farther into the depths of her big house, hiding from the specter of her former lover.

I eventually coaxed her out in my best German, *"Astrid, es ist der Steve. Ich habe mein tot gefaelscht und denn verschwunden. Es tut mir leid, ich habe dir geschreckt."* (Hey, it's just me. I faked my death and disappeared. I'm sorry to have scared you.)

But she never got over her panic. The formerly composed and regal professor was now a little girl wrapped in an oversized sweater. "Two men in green uniforms came looking for you the year before," she said. "They asked if I had seen you, and although I said no, I saw them later in the woods behind the house." She refused to meet my eyes.

"When the men came," she said, "I knew you were in trouble from something crazy you would have done. And now you are miraculously here."

I told her what had happened, about the NRF, and the ice of Lake Michigan. I explained that Steven was dead, and that I was Nathan. But she shook her head and pulled further into herself, into her sweater.

I told her I needed to go back home, to the United States, and then she perceived a way out. She left the room and came back with a wad of cash. She seemed relieved to be rid of me, and I knew this was the last time I would ever see her. And it was, except in the loneliness that I could feel pervaded her life, perhaps some pleasant memories of me, but more likely a few nightmares.

* * *

The Mystagogue

There is a lack of nostalgia to the refrain of this number
Back back back at the removal of a pig

I am the wizard of blown out bellies
I am the phrase maker
You may rent

Scarlet scarlet

Send
Them
Music
Paint their bellies with your gun

—From the Nexalistic Revolutionary Front (NRF)
Documents by Nathan T. Stanfield (NTS)
a.k.a. Steven Kubacki, 1979

* * *

During the long flight home from Germany, I considered what to do next. My first priority was to connect with my co-conspirators. I'd brought them into the NRF, so it was my responsibility to dismantle it and set them free.

I landed in New York and went right to Princeton, knocking on Paul's door in the dead of night. He was shocked to see me since he'd been imagining me in France, receiving my white hat and learning to kill.

Instead, I announced that I could never kill, and was therefore terminating the NRF, effective immediately. At first, Paul protested and stared at me. He was disappointed in me. He had such high hopes and clung to the lofty ambitions of our revolution. He refused to abandon his chance to change the world and argued passionately that night for his vision of the NRF and its celestial mission. I was dashing a future that would certainly be far more impactful than the one of a minister in a church with a limited audience and some books on theology and philosophy that few would read.

I told him about the visions I'd had of the future, the revelations of what the NRF would actually become. Instead of being horrified, Paul thought that the visions might represent the future God wanted—the difficult birth of a theologically-enlightened, meritocracy based, democratic nation. The Book of Revelation, which was part of the Christian canon, he said, described human carnage like what I saw as part of the path to paradise. What if we were meant to be the instruments of prophecy? He saw no reason why, with the technology and science of the day, we couldn't bring about purely democratic governments and business institutions. "We will be blessed as martyrs," he told me.

We debated through the night, two brothers taking apart the nature of evil, the value of theology. Paul argued for the necessity of violence. I tried to take the position of C.S. Lewis, a Christian theologian Paul admired. In his book *The Great Divorce*, Lewis describes what happens when humans turn away from the infinite, from love, God, from the totality of existence. The result is always a vast contraction of the self to fixed attachments of hate, envy, and depression—the burning and icy-cold isolation that is referred to as hell.

I was not going to create hell, neither for myself nor others.

Paul only smiled at my pronouncement. Sensing that we had reached a kind of understanding, I reached into my red backpack—the same one I'd rescued from the Paris train station—and found a bottle of Cognac I had procured then.

Paul smiled and bowed his head. "Let us pray."

"Let us meditate," I replied.

We spent the remainder of the night exploring alternative timelines to the NRF. We saw how from the ashes of our failed revolution, a new timeline based on love, community, healing, and freedom was unfolding, maybe even a reborn NRF. By sunrise, we'd both accepted we would need to take separate paths—more legitimate paths—to make the world a better place. Paul would continue at seminary and become a spiritual leader. My path was still unknown. Would I continue as Nathan, or return to Steven? The course of action would take time to unfold.

Time, we acknowledged as we embraced and said goodbye, was the thing we had not given to the current NRF. Our rush to act and the secretiveness with which we'd surrounded ourselves had possibly poisoned our goal before it even started.

"Transparency is not enough," Paul reminded me as I prepared to leave. "We need to be radically transparent."

I embraced him before I set out again. We were not typically huggers, but physical touch felt important in this moment. From a distance we had already touched each other's hearts.

* * *

Spiritual Cannibalism

Oh

the

wish

to

eat

you

is

strong

even

though

I cannot

finish

you

—From the Nexalistic Revolutionary Front (NRF)
Documents by Nathan T. Stanfield (NTS)
a.k.a. Steven Kubacki, 1979

* * *

While I was at Paul's, I called Walter in Chicago and Alex in Michigan. Alex was gracious, and perhaps not surprised. He welcomed me back, wished me luck, and said goodbye.

Walter's reaction was a heartbreaking lack of reaction. He heard my story and what I had to say, and then dismissed it, and me. Before the Foreign Legion debacle, I had wondered if he had abandoned the Right Arm and the NRF. He was trying to build a legitimate future in the world of finance. Regarding plans Paul and I had discussed to redirect the NRF, Walter's engagement seemed half-hearted, and he offered few suggestions. I could tell his heart wasn't in it. In some way, I suspected he had been ambivalent since the day I disappeared. Walter could be a brilliant artist, writer, and entrepreneur, but like many a radical young man, when his college playtime was done and it was time to fit into the system, he wasn't about to miss a beat on the path to become another money-hoarding, golf-playing CEO.

Walter was quick to remind me that a private investigator was still looking for me, and not only that, but he'd heard from James about receiving a letter from my mother directly, suggesting that she visit and—in his words—"interrogate" James. I wonder if Walter had told James about the conspiracy; after all, they were peas from the same privileged pod.

I wished him luck. I had other concerns at the moment.

* * *

What I admire about Kubacki is his capacity to cross bridges people never do. Then, on the other side, burn them, if ever they existed.

—Letter from Paul to Walter, 1979

* * *

I'd called Richard before I called Walter, and I worried about his response. Or rather, I worried because he'd had almost nothing to say when I told him about the Foreign Legion failure and the dissolution of the NRF. Although he'd been the last person to learn of the conspiracy, he was by far the most committed, and his silence struck me as ominous. He knew enough about everything to make my life hell, but probably his own also.

I needed to see Richard in person.

Although Paul had given me money for a plane, I chose to hitchhike across the country. Blooms of cherry trees and daffodils in the early spring were along the sides of many streets, and so the highway beckoned. It was already March, more than a year since Steven disappeared. Would it even be possible to resurrect him? Is that what I wanted?

When I arrived in Madison, I went straight to Richard's house, only to find strangers unpacking their belongings in the kitchen where we'd shared whisky and promises of eternal brotherhood just a few short months ago. Richard hadn't mentioned moving when we talked, and the new tenants—acquaintances of his from the university—mentioned that it had happened quickly. He'd offered them the house just days before.

This seemed like a very bad sign.

The new tenants knew Richard's new phone number, and I took a chance and called him. He sounded cold, distant. I asked to meet him, and he said he would be at the coffee shop, the one where I used to see Natalie.

Of course, Natalie was gone, moved to Vermont just as she said she would. A woman working behind the counter told me that she'd moved away with the coffeeshop owner. She was pregnant with his child.

I'm not sure why that surprised me as much as it did. He'd always been protective of her, jealous of our time. And she did warn me she had terrible taste in men.

Richard arrived and sat down across the table without offering a greeting. He couldn't stay long, he said. He was hosting a party at his new apartment. He did not invite me.

Instead, he asked for money to cover the rent. Trying to ease the tension between us, I gave him just about everything that Paul had given me—almost $700.

I lingered in Madison, crashing on the couch of a mutual friend, hoping to hear from him again, but a week went by in silence. I tried to track him down, tried calling, but he was adept at avoiding me. When the mutual friend mentioned that Richard was dating a woman named Lucy, my concern grew exponentially. Lucy and I had had a brief interlude the fall before when I lived in Madison. If Richard knew about that—and if he'd found out what happened with Amelia—he would be livid.

I finally caught him on the phone one afternoon and asked when he would repay the money he had borrowed. Richard told me he wouldn't pay it back, that he considered it a minimum repayment for all the food I'd eaten and beers he'd paid for while I stayed with him.

I was incensed. I reminded him that I was living underground and had limited ways to make or acquire money, and that I now needed the funds back. I told him that his commitment to the NRF during the earlier times when I was in Madison made any talk of rent specious. He refused to change his mind.

Looking back, I think that Richard was driven by anger and fear. He saw me as a threat to his relationship, to his studies, to his very future. Once, not so long before, he'd been caught up in my spell, the spell of the NRF, and my belief that the systems and powers we despised could be changed. He'd sacrificed himself for that goal, thrown himself into our wild vision and unrealistic plans. Now the spell had broken, and the wildness of his fervency was replaced by the deep emptiness of disappointment and a hurricane of betrayal. He was rightly consumed with resentment and externalizing blame, convinced that I had wasted his time and marred his dreams.

At the time, though, I was too livid to consider any of this. His actions demanded a confrontation, and we had one the next day, right in the middle of the university's student union. I went storming in, hoping to catch Richard after his class. And there he was, in the middle of the busy and expansive room packed with tables, chairs, and chattering students.

We locked eyes and the room seemed to fall away. From a distance, I could see the difference in my friend, my comrade, my brother. His fervor was gone and his passion for change. It was all replaced by rage and contempt.

He leapt up from where he was sitting and charged toward me, hurling obscenities. Through the dull roar in my own ears, I heard him call me a *bastard* and a *fucker*. Within a few inches of my face, he unleashed a malicious exhalation of breath. It was laced with negative energy. Whether it was intentional or a moment of anger, it penetrated my energetic defenses.

To be clear, he never physically touched me. But this was a spiritual and psychological confrontation, one which came with an impact that to this day I am convinced was Richard trying to punish me. Though he would probably have judged it differently, the action seemed to be a release of the me within him. Richard had read the same authors in shamanism as I did and was acquainted with unfriendly encounters that could happen from other dimensions and realities, including soul loss and invasion. He had been building his power, and I felt its full magnitude.

To repel the negative energy, I summoned all of my Nexalist and multidimensional training and experiences. I extracted and dissipated the negative energy into the sky before it could penetrate deeply into me. I succeeded but could still feel the residue that lingered for some time. I said only one word aloud to him. "*Traitor!*"

Vindicated, Richard turned and stalked from the room. The damage was done and might never be reparable. I had to reflect on my responsibility in this. There was a pattern of close friends and lovers abandoning me, so that I felt betrayed, though in many people's lives that dynamic may be common. Clearly, my intensity, relentlessness, and resoluteness, even if compassionate, had a role in that. No doubt, Richard felt the same or more so about me.

It was the last time we ever saw each other until a recent meeting in the early summer of 2024. That went well, I think.

Chapter 13
THE WANDERING MONK

All my life I have been contented to swagger from idiot to idiot.

—From the Nexalistic Revolutionary Front (NRF) Documents by Nathan T. Stanfield (NTS) a.k.a. Steven Kubacki, 1978

By the time I got back to the apartment where I was staying, our mutual friend had already heard about the outburst in the student union, and he asked me to leave as soon as possible. He didn't want to take sides in whatever was brewing between Richard and me.

I wasn't surprised that our friend had heard about the fight, but that he found out so quickly made me pause. I couldn't stay there much longer. Madison often felt like a small gossipy town, and too many people had witnessed our outburst. Remorse washed over my exhaustion. I was still supposed to be in hiding. What if the private investigator was watching Richard? What if he heard about the fight?

Walter's paranoia about the investigator was wearing on me, but the truth is that there were several close calls that spring—some I knew about at the time, and some I'm just starting to understand now.

I had nowhere to go, no friends or compatriots left, and thanks to Richard, almost no money. I went for a walk to clear my head, and once again, the universe intervened in unexpected ways. In the university square, a man I'd never seen before or since handed me a pamphlet promoting a group called the Kali Shugendo in San Francisco.

I took it as a sign. Old habits, as they say, die hard.

As far as I could see, they were a kind of commune with ties to martial arts and Eastern religious practices. That appealed to me, and I wondered if this could be the place to begin the spiritual healing that Paul and I had foreseen: perhaps a different kind of NRF, founded on thoughtfulness, radical transparency, and a different kind of compassion.

At the very least, it would be a quiet place to plan my next move.

* * *

Deep and lasting change comes often externally because we can't so easily control what the world or others do to us. In contrast, it's very hard to internally generate true change, because we are so good at self-deception and rationalization. It can then appear that we change when we did not, or did, but just a little. We should thus thank the universe whenever we are smacked with a two-by-four to the head.

—From the Nexalistic Revolutionary Front (NRF)
Documents by Nathan T. Stanfield (NTS)
a.k.a. Steven Kubacki, 1979

* * *

I set out to hitchhike to San Francisco. I'd made it all the way to Salt Lake City, where I was picked up by a man who seemed odd, but friendly. He liked to talk but didn't say much—his sentences were all vague and rambling, and it was hard for me to draw any kind of story from him. Still, he asked if I was hungry, bought me food from McDonald's, and then asked if I needed a place to sleep.

The weather was cold, and dark was falling, so against my better judgment, I agreed to go with the man and stay in his house. The man drove to a quiet street, one where the houses were scattered and far from each other.

Once we were inside, the man propositioned me for sex. I tried to be polite as I replied that I wasn't interested in that. The man said that was all right and told me that he would make up a bed for me in the guest room. I started to follow him down a dark hallway but stopped when I heard a muffled voice behind a door I was passing. The man had said he lived alone.

Every instinct in my body catapulted to the highest level of alert. I realized that something was dangerous, terribly wrong. "Run," I heard a scared voice inside say. I turned and fled, bumping my backpack against walls in the darkness and fumbling to find the front door. The man was following me, but slowly, asking what I was doing.

I finally got the door handle to open, and as I bolted into the night, I heard a strange voice shout, "You idiot, you forgot to lock the door."

When I reached the street, I ran. "You're a survivalist and a marathon runner," I thought, but my heart pounded in terror, and my breathing labored in the higher altitude. I circled the desert terrain behind the house and ran toward the city light, weaving a kind of semicircular path with my movements. The brambles were high, scratching me, but lit by a full moon, I could avoid most of their thorns. Eventually I found a street and then a housing development. I followed the brightest lights ahead of me to the interstate. After a few minutes of standing nervously with my thumb out, waiting for the odd man to come and possibly shoot me, a tractor trailer stopped, and I climbed aboard, deeply grateful to still be alive.

What had happened in that house? What would have happened? I'll never know for sure, but I believe that night I almost became the dead person everyone thought I already was. There were evils in the world that had little to do with anything political, social, or economic, and certainly had no interest in Nexalism or revolution. If I hadn't been living underground, I think I would have informed the police, but even if I had decided to tell them what had happened there, I had no idea where the house was; I had run many miles.

* * *

In San Francisco, I found the address of the group I sought in a phone book and made my way to the location. I hadn't researched anything about them beyond what the flyer said. I didn't even know why they called themselves Kali Shugendo. Were they somehow tied to the ancient Japanese religion Shugendo, rooted in the traditions of seventh- and eighth-century monks studying a hybrid Shinto and Buddhism for magic and healing? To this day, I don't know. They never explained their origin story, and I never asked. This serendipitous choice of the Shugendo made as much sense as the many others that had chosen me.

I presented the flyer from Madison to the man who appeared to be in charge, who called himself the Kali. The muscular, white, balding, fifty-something man did not resemble the Hindu goddess of death, time, and doomsday, whose name in Sanskrit translates "she who is black." But the name had an ominous and intimidating quality to it, suggesting that the Shugendo was not all that it seemed to be.

Still, the Kali had kind eyes and was a master of making people feel seen and valued. As he gazed at me intently, I felt compelled to tell him all about Steven Kubacki's disappearance on Lake Michigan, and even a little about the NRF and our plans. The only pieces I held back were the names of my co-conspirators.

The Kali rewarded me for my openness with extra attention. I joined the group as a full member, participating in days of long meditations, chanting, and martial arts training with about a dozen other acolytes. Their kindness felt genuine, and I relished their attention and generosity after so many recent betrayals.

I had been part of the Kali Shugendo for about a week when the Kali invited me to be part of a ritual he said had Buddhist roots. A group of mostly women and a few men gathered in a dark room as the Kali led us in a visualization of entering a mandala of life and rebirth. In the concentric circles of the mandala on the floor, I envisioned many gods, goddesses, demons, and animals, all surrounding a large blue Buddha in the center.

After many long minutes or hours of deep meditation, the Kali spoke to the group. He reported that he'd had a vision of my past lives, which he described as intense and interdimensional. To my shock, he declared that I was his long-lost spiritual son, and then he took my hand and helped me to my feet. He led me out of the ceremonial room, leaving everyone else behind, and into an adjacent room I'd never seen before. The decorations here were ornate and luxurious, full of tapestries and soft pillows, and I realized these must be the Kali's private quarters.

He swathed me in ceremonial robes as a group of the most beautiful women devotees of the cult entered, encircling us and chanting.

I was uncomfortable, and yet all of this was familiar. I had done something like this before in a different timeline, or in an earlier life, as the Kali would say. I trusted the universe still, feeling that all this must somehow be all right. And in doing so, I almost altered history again.

The draw of the women of the cult was powerful. The longer I stayed at the Shugendo, the more powerful the draw of all those women and the Kali's repeated assertions that I was his spiritual son and successor became. Clearly, the ancient ascetism of the Shugendo was not central to the Kali's purposes.

I had several dreams during this time of a future where I was at the Kali's side. In one, we stood before a huge crowd in what looked like a football stadium. They were chanting, and it felt like we were leading a movement. Another dream involved erotic rituals with female followers.

Yet nothing like that was actually happening. Before I realized it, weeks had gone by. I was in a fog, caught up in the Kali's spell. It was as if all the work I'd done to recover the lost parts of myself was being undone little by little.

This was not the spiritual path that would lead to a rebirth of a different NRF, but it took a visit from an old ally, the Wandering Monk, to help me see it.

This was a figure I had not seen for many years, but he had appeared in my earliest drawings after I experienced LSD. He always appeared dressed in a robe with a flowing hood, and I saw him as another life from many alternate timelines. Unlike the Dark Monk, the Wandering Monk focused on healing and exploring existence from timeline to timeline, without any interest in power. That was always in conflict with the darker powers that visited me, of course. Indeed, one night with James, long before our ill-fated journey to Europe, I drew a menacing hand in ink, reaching out to grasp the Wandering Monk.

When the Wandering Monk came to me in San Francisco, he offered to take charge of my compromised mind, and I gave him my permission and my gratitude. He helped me resist the women. I never touched any of them, to the disappointment of the Kali. Sex, as most of us learn at some point in our adult lives, can be a binding process that overwhelms any independent thinking.

After my encounter with the Wandering Monk, I started to feel myself again. One evening, I became highly agitated. I felt I was being incorporated into another timeline—one of my own for sure, but not one I had consciously selected. This timeline seemed to be directed by the Kali, and more specifically, by a higher multiverse power that had subjugated the cult leader himself so that he could better control others.

When the Kali began his evening rituals and ceremonies, I resisted. I disassociated and let my mind roam until I found the higher dimensional me, the one with the goatee. His energy was supportive, but it was indifferent to me. He didn't need or want me.

I saw in that moment just how small my actual role in the multiverse is. I like to think I'm special, but I am not. Higher dimensional beings have their own agendas, not mine. What I thought was their interest in me was like the sun warming my body. I can tap into the energy of the sun, but the sun is indifferent to me.

This human-centric fallacy is not unique to me, of course. We are very small players in the cosmos. A blood cell streaming through an artery would, if it could speak, say it was making its own decisions. But it would be unaware that it was part of a larger system that had major sway in its choices. We are part of larger systems and dimensions that have an immense influence on our lives and other events than we would like to admit.

I stayed with the goateed me until he pulled a lever in his glass abode, and in that moment, I felt the Kali's invasion stop. I got up and left the room.

The Kali summoned me to his chamber later that night and demanded to know why I resisted. I told him the truth, the whole truth: that this was not the timeline where I was called to live, and that I had a different purpose, a different path with whatever the NRF would become.

Instead of being upset, he tried to use what I said to manipulate me into becoming his successor. He told me the NRF had been right, and that I must use the Shugendo to wage my war against the dragon.

The Kali was astute and thought he knew how to reach me. But I had the Wandering Monk's guidance as a counter.

A few hours later, I snuck out of the plush room where I'd slept ever since being named the successor. I didn't need a vision to see what was to come of me if I stayed. I wouldn't be able to resist either the Kali's seductive pull of power or the beautiful women forever, but like Frodo in *The Lord of the Rings*, I would eventually be taken over.

And that, I knew from many years of reading the creative writers of great fiction, would induce a wound that would never heal.

The only thing to do, I surmised, was for Steven Kubacki to come back to life; to come home.

* **

Nathan,

I don't give a goddamn whether Alex, Richard, Natalie, Astrid or anyone else in this wretched crew is with me or not. The first rumblings of the Hoax College Days revealed a clear choice. I have made it and so have you. There is not martyrdom here, no sensationalism. The creation of a power base, structured through the political element (Paul), the financial element (Walter), and the ideological element (Steven) is the first phase. . .

It was disgusting, Alex and the others. Don't they realize that your defeat, indeed the defeat of the NRF, would mean their own doom? Didn't they see that they were sacrificing a great purpose — a vision of creating our destinies — on the gross and petty altar of the self?

Didn't they see that the mastery of that self does not arise from security and hedonism, but from total risk?

I know you are with me; indeed, I am with you. Paul is also among us . . .

Andromeda awaits,
Walter Smith

—Letter to Nathan post-reemergence, 1979

I guess I was wrong about Walter. He did care, he continued to believe and appeared committed to a re-visioned future. I guess he wasn't quite ready to accept the everyday banality of being another CEO in the system.

* * *

April 25, 1979

Dear Steve:

It's been a long time since I last wrote to you, but actually nothing much has happened in the interim. Life and things around the house go on pretty much the same. . .

I haven't heard from James for a long time—after I wrote him at least three short letters. I guess he's too busy or just doesn't want to bother—but I do want to see your poems and will, one way or another.

My search for you continues, and I save a little each week so I can do some things to find you—I have given up hope of Randolph doing anything—and anyway it was gratis. Actually, he found out nothing concrete—not a single thing—all is purely circumstantial and speculative theory. This Friday, John J and I will be going out to Holland—I don't know what kind of reception we'll get if any from the people we will visit. . . and then, of course, a visit to the lake where you spent some time. . . I will stay on until Monday and then go on to Madison. First to try to locate the girl on TV who was given a hard time by the fire department in feeding her baby, and where I saw you standing in the doorway of her apartment. This was in January, and it's taken me some time to get the finances together to permit me to go, but I am very optimistic. I'll also mostly likely drop by to see Richard Turner — although I'm not sure what for.

Otherwise, all goes on pretty well, just that I miss you so very much and nothing seems right or complete anymore — something is missing, and that missing link that kinda gets me all together is you and knowing that you are all right. I guess that's all I really need to know — that you are well and safe.

Love,

Mom

Chapter 14
KEEPING THE SILENCE

Asshole reporters prying, suspicious, credulous, made the more insignificant in their obsession for validation, pose tricky questions, waiting to see if the prodigy slips and is exposed. Black and white, right and wrong, the periphery mistaken as center — the pluck of ambition shunned, my entrails streaming over the wisdom of my brothers — blow them away, tell the truth; these are not people of ruthless compassion.

Artists are self-conceited. The art of survival and the art of evasion, I mastered both. Food? Money? Identification? The procurement of those is not left to indiscretion and accident, otherwise starvation results. Private detectives were hired; the FBI and Interpol investigated without consequence. Pride? You better believe I'm proud. Pride in what, who. . . Was it me? Pride in a lurking darkness unexplained and unmanifested, pride that tightens my throat and threatens to gag my efforts to breathe, to speak. Yes. . . I guess it's pride. Fooled this stinking world and fooled myself in thinking I could become that revolutionary. . . If only I knew how to resolve this conundrum of emergence. . . I chant: may the duality of amnesia and recollection conclude without resolution and my mind assent to contradiction as a basis for the visible and invisible.

—Personal papers of Steven Kubacki, 1979

* * *

I blinked in the flash of yet another camera capturing the image of me, thin and wide-eyed and wearing a striped shirt I don't recognize having purchased. In the picture, taken by a local photographer from *The Greenfield Reporter* and shared via wire service with dozens of papers across the country, I am in my father's living room, and he leans toward me smiling, with tears in his eyes.

Curiously, my mother is in none of the news reports from that time—no pictures, no quotes. My father was always the one to step forward, gregarious and full of the need for attention and recognition. Yet it is my mother who saved me, in her way. She is the reason I came home. It was her relentless pursuit of me that made an underground existence impossible.

By the time I left San Francisco, I knew my time as Nathan T. Stanfield had come to an end. The NRF, and the financial support that came with it, was gone. Natalie was gone. Nathan Stanfield had no purpose, no comrades, nothing to help him face the relentless pressure of being discovered.

With the help of the Wandering Monk, I had discovered that I could withstand great deprivation. I could see myself as a Han Shan, writing poetry on cave walls in the wild mountains of China, or as a solitary robed man running barefoot in Tibet. But I also saw that continuing to roam the world was not my solution in this timeline. In other places and other dimensions, I could wander like the monk. I could disappear. I could sacrifice for love or for war. But in this world, I had a mission of service, with or without the NRF. I was born to heal and help people and this planet in spite of my many flaws and inadequacies. Being a wanderer, or too monk-like, would not help me to carry out my mission of service.

The darkness that pursued me, I now realized, was a quantum set of superimposed timelines involving rage, fear, and sadness. Over the many years, I had projected onto them my anxiety and insecurities, making them seem threatening and dangerous, when in fact, they were also trying to instruct and guide me. Perhaps now I could integrate with them.

I started hitchhiking east, crossing the entire country to make it back to my mother, my family. I would be safe there, protected from the glare of the spotlights and questions I anticipated every time I closed my eyes.

* * *

"Let's start with what we know," says the man in uniform. He opens his notepad and looks expectantly at me.

We are seated in what wants to be an interrogation room with a bare table and bare walls, but is really a hotel room. Coffee and a lit cigarette perfume the air. The detective glowers, but my family is there as well. My mother leans toward me, listens in anticipation.

I am silent.

"Okay," sighs the detective, eyeing me with thinly veiled annoyance. "I guess I'll go first, since you're not feeling very talkative."

He checks his notepad. "So, you left your apartment the morning of February 19. Your roommate didn't see or hear you leave, but states when he woke up you were already gone. A couple of townsfolk saw you headed toward Holland State Park, but no one saw you once you actually got there. Based on where your belongings were found you likely skied"—the notepad rustles—"northwest, in the direction of Tunnel Park. Do I have that right?"

Like a Buddhist monk, deep in meditation, I do not respond. My mother takes my hand and squeezes it encouragingly.

"You say you fell through the ice," grunts the investigator. "Where was that exactly? Because the search party found no evidence of a breach near where your belongings were found."

Silently, I stare straight ahead. The secret is to not make eye contact.

"All right." The man leans back in his chair, his badge glinting in the harsh overhead lights. "What happened next—after you fell through the ice?"

Like the wisps of smoke trailing from the investigator's neglected cigarette, memories curl through my mind. I keep them to myself.

"Son," he says, aware that something is happening behind my eyes, but unable to glean it. "You can't hide from this forever. People will want to know what happened to you. And I'm not some reporter you can bullshit. I'm a county sheriff, and I've driven a long way to come talk to you on my own time, so why don't you think real hard before just shaking your head at me. A lot of people back home have questions, and I think you owe them some answers. They put their lives on the line looking for you, son."

"I'm sorry officer, my son, he—"

"No need to apologize ma'am, and this isn't an interrogation. You son's a grown man now. He ought to be able to stand on his own and tell the truth."

"You're right, you're right. I'm sorry."

"That's all right. Now, about that man who says he picked you up the day you called your aunt from that payphone—he says you gave him a false name. Nathan, Nathan Stanfield. You ever go by that alias, son? Think real hard before shaking your head at me now."

"I don't remember."

"You don't remember what? Using a fake name? Hitchhiking?"

"I don't remember anything other than—"

"Yeah, yeah—you were cold, it was dark. I've heard all that already."

"That's all I remember."

"I don't believe you, son. And neither do my men back home."

"Officer, please—"

"Ma'am, respectfully, it's my job to know a liar, and your son is lying right now. Now, listen here, Steve, we put a lot of effort into that search—helicopters, planes, divers. People put their lives on the line—going beneath the ice looking for you. Do you understand that?"

"Yes."

"I don't think you do, else you'd stop lying and tell me the truth. Who is Nathan Stanfield? Where were you? What were you doing all that time you were missing?"

* * *

March 15, 1979

Dear George,

First of all, both John J and I wish to thank you for your excellent support and the services that you have given to us in our search for Steven. We realize the limitations placed upon you by our inability to reimburse you financially and that you have, most generously and tirelessly, given us aid during this very trying period, assistance that we could not have gotten elsewhere.

Pursuant to our telephone conversation and after deep reflection. . . We do not wish to have his name registered with the *federal agency (Justice Department) in Washington, DC, as a "known" affiliate with subversive and/or terrorist organizations or persons. We do not know for a fact or in actual truth that this is so. Granted he was pursuing research in this area, but that is all we know for sure. All the rest is projected purely on theory and assumption. . . We do not in any way wish to negate your investigative direction, methods, or purpose. It was in every way to locate Steven. But since at this point in time (approximately fourteen months since his disappearance and no sign of his remains in Lake Michigan), there have been no definitive points of fact, we do not in any way want to make Steven's return at some future date an impossibility, his return as a law-abiding citizen of this country with full rights and privileges accorded him with no mark against him as a supposed subversive.*

Irene Pegg

* * *

If people knew the truth of where I had been—of what I had done—that would have forever limited and defined my future. Most likely, I wouldn't have been admitted into a psychology PhD program and my potentials most likely not realized. Worse, the true story would also have forever affected my fellow conspirators and perhaps deny the dreams they still wanted to fulfill. Some of us still harbored the desire to develop a new kind of Nexalist movement, while others wanted to lead "normal" lives without drama or the spotlight.

If I constructed a story that was just simple enough, and just hollow enough, to allow others to fill in the missing parts themselves,

I and my co-conspirators would have a chance to start new chapters in our lives.

I wasn't going to be gobbled up by the system. The NRF might be dead, but I was still a Nexalist, and if I could develop a way to outsmart the system and attain a way and means to still help the world, so be it.

Oddly, somewhere along the winding road back to Massachusetts, I conversed with a man in a truck stop. He told me a story he heard about a man who woke up by the side of the road in Seattle on a Thursday afternoon with no idea how he got there. The man—I found out later his name was Richard Edwards—lived in Salt Lake City and had left for work on Wednesday morning like any other day. Twenty-nine hours later, he was in Seattle, wearing the same clothes and carrying all of the cash he'd had when he left his house, but his identification was missing. His truck was in a canyon back in Utah.

Could it be that simple? Could having no answer be the answer I needed? Amnesia?

I don't remember anything about the trip from San Francisco to Great Barrington. I'm assuming here that I hitchhiked. I may have taken a bus. My mind has blocked out everything except Richard Edwards' story, which became my story.

Becoming Steven Kubacki again required levels of discipline, secrecy, and silence. Nathan T. Stanfield had never been good at any of those things, but he'd never had the motivation of a police department investigation, nor days of relentless reporters asking questions. A lack of silence now had immediate consequences, the possible punishment of my comrades and brothers, the risk to myself.

There was urgency in this secret, and that made all the difference.

* * *

I see myself stealing back to my father's house in the dead of night. I avoid the front yard, where camera crews still camp like carrion birds waiting for fresh morsels. It has been eight days since my amazing and mysterious reemergence, and little new information has emerged. Soon, I hope they will fly away, give up their determination to feast on me until there is nothing left.

I slip past them unnoticed and enter the basement through a low window. A radio in my room plays the news of the day, its volume loud enough to be heard by anyone who might pass by the door at the top of the stairs, drowning out the lack of other noise my absence would reveal. Switching it off, I go to the couch and empty the contents of the backpack I've retrieved from the grassy field near Great Barrington. My writings and journals spill out.

I shuffle through the pile. Some of the documents are entirely familiar, while others seem to have been written by a mad prophet.

"I move onward into the unremembered. I speak of places extant but not here."

"In the drawl of deliberation, I mention many things that evanesce and then without permission dig their own little grubby holes."

"Inside those holes are fragmentary meanings—tools to accomplish both the mean and magnanimous tasks of Party intentionalities—these germinate then bloom or fester on the NRF assembly line of unplanned systemic change, in this case—my departure from Hawaii and resurrection."

I close my eyes and see a pyramid wreathed in snakes. I see the hinge at the bottom of the lake, and the rift between the layers of ice and snow where new worlds can be accessed like so many doors in a hallway. Waves break on the shores of a tropical island, laden with cherry blossoms as red as teardrops of blood.

I recall a voice but not my own. *"This planet is dying. We are sending you and others back to retrieve a living knowledge in a space that your mind cannot yet comprehend. This living knowledge will unfold as you get older so you can fulfill the mission, when you have parachuted down to your Earth to be born."*

A knock on the basement door ends my respite. My father appears at the top of the stairs with a sandwich on a plate. I hastily tuck the papers beneath a blanket and rise to break bread in the everyday world.

* * *

Life returned, day by day, to something that resembled Steven Kubacki's past. I lived with my father but saw my mother almost daily. I got a job in a local plastics factory so that I could save some money for whatever came next. I kept my head down as much as possible, avoided nosy neighbors and reporters, and focused my mind in the present reality, no matter how devastating it was.

Those were not easy months, though they may have seemed like it on the outside. Seeing my mother's joy was wonderful. By connecting with my family and receiving the welcome of a community I thought despised me, I felt valued and appreciated in ways I'd never felt before.

Yet still, the depression was deep. Nathan T. Stanfield, counterculture revolutionary man on the run, was gone, and I was back to "little Stevie" living with his parents, regressing to the dependence of a son, a worker, a cog in the wheel of the system I'd been trying to break not long before.

* * *

May 12, 1979

Dear Mrs. Pegg:

I am certainly glad for you that Steven has safely returned, and I do understand about how he and his father must feel hassled by the press at the present time. But their interest is usually short-lived.

Some of the things you were able to tell me do tend to put the case into the category of an ordinary amnesia, but then there are strange possibilities that someday he may wish to explore. In any event, he may wish to find out, privately, just what did go on, without having to deal with psychiatrists.

My own interest is in UFO close-encounter cases, and I'm writing on the slight possibility that there may have been that sort of an involvement. There are ways we use of getting the information from the unconscious mind that may be of some help in Steven's case. I'll enclose an explanation of how the "pendulum technique" works, and a questionnaire that he may find helpful is appended below (see instructions).

Please extend my best regards to Steven when you see him.

Sincerely,
James A. Harder, PhD

* * *

August 1979

"This is the last time I'm going to make this drive, son. I know by now you're not going to tell me the truth. I just wanted to come out here one last time and look you in the eye to tell you I don't believe your story and I wish you'd reconsider. Amnesia isn't as simple as you're making it out to be."

The Deputy stares across the table at the young man, trying to glean a reaction to what he has just said. When the young man offers none, he sips his coffee.

"I saw a UFO once—out on the lake. Did you know that?"

The young man shakes his head.

"Ah, why would you? Never told anyone anyhow. It was like a bright light—only it kept changing shape and moving this way and that. Came right out of nothing—right out of thin air. I lost three hours that night—can't account for them."

He takes another sip.

"Truth be told, when you first went missing and we couldn't find any trace of you—I thought of that night. Silly, I know. There are a thousand simpler explanations. But that's just where my mind went."

"Deputy?" says the young man, breaking his silence, "What color was it? The light?"

"Color?"

The young man nods.

"Can't say for sure—red, maybe. I think about that night a lot these days, son. It's gotten harder and harder to pretend it didn't happen. I guess I was hoping when you turned up after all those months gone, you might—I don't know—have some answers that might satisfy my own curiosity. But then you gave your cockamamie amnesia excuse, and I knew you were full of shit."

"They'll come back for you, Deputy."

"What?"

"They'll be back. Once they've taken an interest in you, they don't forget—even if you have."

* * *

What does a man do after he has disappeared, reappeared? After he has set out to save the world and touched corners and pieces of the universe usually off limits to humans, and then comes back to Earth?

On the surface, what comes next may all seem mundane.

A letter arrived from Hope College, rescinding the honorary diploma they'd awarded me. If I wanted a bachelor's degree, I needed to go back and finish the nine credit hours still required of me, which I did by attending a few classes at the University of Massachusetts, Amherst.

I traveled once to Vermont to see Natalie. She was a single mother by then—the coffeeshop owner was out of the picture, and not surprisingly, she never explained why. She was surprised when I told her that I loved her and had always loved her. She smiled a little and told me I was gallant, but too adventuresome, too radical for her now. She wanted to settle down and raise her child, put the mysteries and wanderlust behind her.

I got letters from Walter now and then, but it was never the same. His written words carried the promises of radical ideas, but I had learned the hard way that Walter was all talk. He liked hearing about my post NRF escapades, but I wonder if he was also making sure I never blew his cover as the facilitator of my disappearance. His corporate and finance friends would not like that. I visited him many times in Chicago, Washington, DC, Amsterdam, and Milan.

Paul and I wrote many letters to each other through that summer and for years to come. We even visited in person a few times. We kept alive our dream of breaking free, working together for something greater or bigger. For many years, the radical Christian and I kept the ideas of the NRF alive in some nonviolent way, dreamed of revolutions together, held each other accountable for not falling into the traps of the complacent world.

Over time, the fervency of my comrades faded, along with any possibility that we would get together again in some way to combine our intellects and energies. That unique confluence of events, an alignment of the stars that brought them together, did not replicate itself.

On the surface, it must seem like we all had become quite complacent, absorbed into the system we claimed to despise. Yet I choose to see deeper than that—I find the praxis of my own choices and actions, the motivations in each move I made, from financier to linguist to psychologist to multiverse explorer to professor to writer.

It's true that the events and ideas surrounding my disappearance receded as time went by. I started dating a woman who worked in a convenience store, and later we worked in a nearby plastic factory. It was the first significant relationship I'd had since reemergence that lasted more than a month or two. Her name was Susan, but it did not endure. Then I met Sheila through Walter. She lived near Springfield, and I moved in with her.

Perhaps the goals and missions of the Right Arm were still in my mind when Sheila suggested that I could get a job in an office, rather than continuing with manual labor. I'd finished my classes at Hope by then, and I was ambitious. Perhaps that's why I never saw getting a job at an investment banking firm as my selling out, not in the way that college-aged Steven certainly would have judged it. All I knew was that factory work bored me out of my mind, and it was time to explore another option. I would treat it as a study in humanity, just like when I'd worked in the Atlanta café run by the Christians.

The job didn't last long—I was too much of a loose cannon for the buttoned-up world of banking. I was reprimanded by my manager for dancing too wildly at a company Christmas party. But it opened other doors, and I started to walk through them—specifically, to return to academia. I was convinced by a professor in German at the University of Massachusetts to enroll in a master's program in German, with a tuition waiver and a teaching assistantship. I really wasn't interested in German but saw Teaching English to Speakers of Other Languages (TESOL) as a way to support myself and my desire for international travel. I eventually transferred to Ohio University, but my direction still never quite felt right. Linguistics, while interesting since it was so fundamental to being a human being, felt too esoteric, too ivory-tower, too detached from interacting with people.

That realization led me to a PhD in clinical psychology at the University of New Mexico. If anyone had told twenty-three-year-old Steven Kubacki, founder of the Nexalistic Revolutionary Front, that for many decades he would find his calling as a revolutionary psychotherapist, pressing individuals and mental health professionals to expand their knowledge and perspectives about interpersonal and emotional reactions, he would have rolled on the floor laughing—or perhaps stormed out of the room in disgust. My early interactions with the ideas of psychology had not impressed me—they seemed futile compared to the systemic studies of philosophy, spirituality, economics, politics, and sociology.

Within a decade of my reappearance, though, the direction of my attention had swung almost 180 degrees. Instead of focusing on big picture plans and ways to change the systems that controlled human beings, I shifted to a dedicated emphasis on how to help and improve the lives of individuals—adults, children, couples, and groups. Change in one area without the other, I'd come to realize, was illusionary.

A person can't change systems without changing themselves first. The political, economic, spiritual, and psychological lessons I learned from the thwarted NRF revolution, and the knowledge I received from other non-ordinary or otherworldly sources, continue to transform me and influence my life mission: to take the world by storm by reenvisioning what humans can amazingly become.

Perhaps a bit wiser and a bit more mature, I have been and am still ready and willing to throw the dice again.

* * *

Misfits and alienated of the world hear me. Don't allow yourselves to be put out to pasture. Don't be marginalized by "going it alone" under the misdirection of extreme individualism and socially marketed narcissism. Your power in numbers will become dissipated. Society's capacity to control is sophisticated and deceptive in catching and subduing the unwary and isolated. They want to transform you into tame and obedient products. But don't think that by recognizing how society controls your life it will be any easier. The status quo will come after you to undermine you any way it can—psychologically, interpersonally, economically, politically, and culturally. Havens, secret societies, and caves can provide temporary sanctuary, but the status quo is relentless in the rooting out and undermining of perceived threats to its control.

. . . It is important to know that we misfits are not so much different from those who have been incorporated into the system. The difference is we can see the bullshit and the attempts of the culture to make us depressed, anxious, compliant, addicted, distracted, and mentally ill. They fear us because we are anomalies of near health. They want us ill and fucked up. Otherwise, how would they be able to control us? They want to make us become like them—accept our lots with resignation and even with manipulated glee, like the powerless clones who loved Big Brother. George Orwell's book 1984 wasn't far from the truth regarding our enslavement. Still, though we misfits—we anomalous—can see, who will translate that sight into concerted activity? Who will participate and join in the dialectics of disaster and rejuvenation? Who will be accountable and responsible for liberating humankind, so we truly unfold our infinite potential as both individuals and as a species? Let us burn the bridges to bondage. Let us napalm the false and disguised prisons that control our minds . . .

—From the Nexalistic Revolutionary Front (NRF)
Documents by Nathan T. Stanfield (NTS)
a.k.a. Steven Kubacki, 1978

Epilogue
POST-DISAPPEARANCE

High up in the Cascade Mountain range is one of my favorite mountain hikes. Just a short drive from my home, it's an arduous climb. Over the years, it's been a perfect place to train for other climbs, like nearby Mt. Rainier or in the Cordillera Blanca in the Peruvian Andes. But more than that, a "secret" and typically deserted trail to summit has been the place where I go to connect with energies and beings from other dimensions, meditate, and journey in the multiverse. As I hike the trail, I at times engage in being in two or more "places" at the same time, which I call constructive disassociation, in contrast to maladaptive disassociations like those in post-traumatic stress disorder or dissociative identity disorder. It's a kind of pilgrim's-path-meets-convergence zone along the mountain's ridge.

I was on my favorite mountain when I first realized it was time to write this book.

For more than forty-five years, I tried to quell the conversation about my disappearance.

As a graduate student in psychology in the late 1980s, I came across my own name in textbooks describing unexplainable cases of amnesia. I immediately wrote to the book publisher and demanded that my story be removed. I had not given permission for it to be shared, I argued, and I was never diagnosed with amnesia by a licensed psychologist or medical doctor. The publishers complied.

In all of these years, I never agreed to an interview or talked on the record with anyone about what happened. I even turned down a contract from a producer who wanted to make a movie from my story. When television shows like *Ancient Aliens* called, asking for my version of the story, I declined—or ignored the messages all together. The circle of those who knew what really happened to Nathan T. Stanfield was small—a few close friends, my ex-wife, my fiancée, and a couple of colleagues. I worried how it would affect my professional reputation as a therapist. A few clients did discover my disappearance on the internet, but no one ever left my practice because of it. I worried about unnecessary exposure and the attention that the disappearance would generate.

As the internet expanded into daily life and constant communication, my ability to control the narrative weakened. The publicly available parts of my story have, as they say, gone viral, with millions of people viewing videos that speculate on what *really* happened.

None of them know what really happened. But people all over the world imagined different scenarios for what happened to me. Their speculation—their wonder—has created innumerable alternate timelines wherein all manner of strange and fantastic things happened during my missing fifteen months.

The memoir I've told here is the story of what happened, in which I faked my death in order to start a revolution, and in the process opened doors to commune with interdimensional beings and explore versions of myself across the multiverse. My experience on the ice in Lake Michigan has been hypothesized as an abduction, but that's not what happened. Traditional spiritual people—ancient and modern—might have described it as being with spirits, power animals, angels, gods, goddesses, Buddhas, heavens, hells, imaginary lands, and more.

The members of the NRF were together an incredible brain trust, but we missed the most basic, obvious truth: that the vision for the NRF had fundamental flaws. The Nexalistic Revolutionary Front could never succeed because we were not killers. Nathan T. Stanfield had a mission to sacrifice empathy and compassion, and he failed to accomplish it. Steven Kubacki could not sacrifice his humanity.

The revolution of the NRF failed and thank goodness it did. The events during my disappearance, and many before, were extreme. Our intentions were good, and I still believe today that our plans for political and economic democracy were meant to bring about a better world. But in 1978, we were wild-eyed idealists hell-bent on bringing about change.

Rebellious actions that sprang from individual anger only took me so far, but I could not become the Left Arm as we had so idealistically envisioned it. I could not change who I was. In the end, the individual was stronger than the system.

From the perspective of systemic change, obviously we did very little. We didn't kill anybody. We didn't plant bombs or destroy property. I didn't recruit or train a guerilla army. I came close to the edge of the abyss, as I had many times before, but I could not compel myself to go over it.

But from a personal standpoint, those fifteen months that Steven Kubacki was dead and Nathan Stanfield roamed the world changed more than simply my life. They continue to ripple. Without Nathan, I wouldn't have connected to the multiverse in the way I did. I would not have gained the knowledge and information to expand my consciousness, thereby discovering new ways to move beyond my individual and crippling history of pain and find better ways to be helpful to others. I had incredible experiences: interdimensional immersions, romances, drama, philosophical and ideological debates. I gained insights about humanity and existence itself. I wrote wildly, creating a playground to work out my anxieties, grandiosity, lust, ruthlessness, traumas, sarcasm, and devaluations by others. I immersed myself in darkness through my encounters with the Dark Monk, and in doing so, saw its limitations, untruths, and usefulness, thereby emancipating myself from it, from power as truth in contrast to love as truth. I became an advocate of nonviolence, transparency, and ardent communication.

I needed those experiences to show me that rage is not the answer, that anger and hate will not change anything. I needed to understand the difference between thinking about systemic change, growing frustrated by what I saw happening around me, and praxis—actually acting on my dreams and theories, being willing to take risks and gamble everything for what I believed. I needed a clearer sense of the darkness that pervades humankind, the planet, and existence.

I've said before that the NRF was not just an experiment, but was my destiny, and forty-five years later, I stand by that. The attention this story is receiving now has opened doors for me to take everything I've learned—about individual change, about the multiverse, about darkness and light—and bring it back to the systemic level. Society has swung into a place where all of the attention is on individual politics, personality, and people-based change. But the systems are more broken than ever.

It's time to bring Nexalism or something like it back to the bigger-picture issues of the day. Changing the individual without also working to change the system creates the illusion of difference, but nothing is actually new. I'm convinced that the story of my disappearance needs to be told now so that it can help society and other individuals to be emancipated from the darkness and embrace a positive well-being.

From the moment I decided to reemerge, I knew that the information I received before, during, and after my disappearance from the multiverse could not be made sense of until I matured as a human being and so could then be made useful. The past forty-five years have been a long journey of maturing emotionally, interpersonally, intimately, psychologically, socially, cognitively, academically, aesthetically, nutritionally, physically, and energetically (my modern word for what others would call the spiritual) with lots of conflict and drama.

LSD experiences, some of which are narrated in this memoir, occurred during special occasions and encounters. This was in keeping with the tribal societies I had studied who used psychedelics for specific, often spiritual, purposes. Though there are numerous experiences described here, in truth these were far apart and were not on any regular basis. While they were without a doubt revelatory, many of my experiences in the multiverse were and have been drug-free.

At age seventy, I am now ready to deliver what I could not before and what I misinterpreted and misunderstood during my disappearance. Indeed, I have now come full circle—from systems thinker and revolutionary, to individually focused psychologist, to an integration of the two. I am ready to integrate and share my knowledge, training, and experiences to not only help the individual, but also to help improve civilization at a systemic level.

Very recently Paul has been in touch, has read this manuscript, and has expressed his fervent hopes about how Christianity and the multiverse can guide humanity, Nexalistic action can overcome repressive action, and a planetary economics and governance can become a reality. Paul himself has written an amazing book on an alternative history of the United States, in which the original 1776 revolution fails and the British win, but where later a new revolution occurs led by Frederick Douglas, resulting in a truly democratic Constitution that is for the people and not the rich and powerful.

* * *

Steven and Nathan's Last Adventure

"Has he been found?"

"No, the search hasn't come up with anything other than a tent with a lot of his gear inside."

"No tracks from the summit?"

"It's been very windy the last few days, and blowing snow would erase any tracks. There are some deep crevasses nearby. We went down as far as we could but saw nothing. Some may extend to the crater's core."

"He's over a hundred, probably demented. How in the fuck did he get up there?"

"He's old and not in the best of health, but he's always training. Those weekly rituals with the multiverse, the mountain, the fairies, and who the fuck knows what. Maybe lots of caffeine. When we climbed together, he said large amounts of caffeine cured high-altitude sickness."

"Yeah, okay. How's his wife doing?"

"She's weirdly upbeat. She's not worried about him. Says he wanted to camp out around Mt. Rainier. She thought it was silly, but he was uncontrollable, willful, and always had been."

"We found some writing in his tent, not much, but here it is, if you want to share it with her."

'They have come for me. I see them above, though above would be inaccurate—they are all around me. I remember that I once wanted to discover immortality. I'm not sure I ever will, but with them, who knows?'

"There are a few sentences crossed out so they can't be read—just blocks of ink. Then he continues."

'They called me here, and with their help, I made it to the top. I have done all I can for the world. I have accomplished my mission on planet Earth. Now for a new adventure. I can feel the energy and the brightness. All I need is to walk out of this tent.'

ACKNOWLEDGMENTS

I would first like to acknowledge Dylan James Quarles because of his significant contributions; without him, this book would not be possible. I would like to express my thanks for major editing by Beth Jusino, who guided the rewriting so it could become a publishing reality. I want to thank all my friends for their encouragement and guidance, in particular Michael Hesley and Christopher Matthais, and especially my son Alexander. Special thanks to my fiancée, Diane Browning.

ABOUT THE AUTHORS

Steven Kubacki, PhD, is a clinical psychologist, mountaineer, and former academic professor, department chair, clinical director, and Fulbright-Hays Scholar, whose name became internationally known after his mysterious disappearance near Lake Michigan in 1978. After vanishing without a trace for fifteen months, Kubacki reappeared with no memory of the lost time—an event that has fueled decades of speculation, conspiracy theories, and viral internet fascination.

Despite media attention, Kubacki remained silent about his disappearance for over four decades. Now, in his long-awaited memoir, he offers a firsthand account of the mystery that captivated millions. Drawing from his professional background in psychology, Kubacki examines his own experience through scientific, philosophical, economic, political, and metaphysical lenses.

He is also the co-author of *Meta-Mathematical Foundations of Existence*, a theoretical exploration of mathematics, consciousness, and cosmology. He currently resides in Seattle, Washington.

Visit him online at www.stevenkubacki.com.

Dylan James Quarles is a bestselling novelist and a 2021 Best Indie Book Award (BIBA) winner for his most recent novel, *There Be Monsters*. His *Ruins of Mars* series has sold more than 100,000 copies, and his *Secret History of Port Townsend* series has been optioned for film. Thanks to his faithful fan base, Quarles has garnered hundreds of glowing reviews. In addition to writing,

Quarles is a regular guest on podcasts exploring conspiracies, popular culture, and more.

Visit him online at www.djqfiction.com.

P.S.

Please check out my website, www.stevenkubacki.com, if you have comments or questions on this book or if you have interest in excerpts from future books: *The Multiverse Guides Humanity*, *The Infinite Personality and Sane Society*, and *Planetary Economics and Governance for Earth, Moon, and Mars*. You can also follow me on podcasts about the book and across a wide range of topics relevant to the Good Life and improving the world. You can find them by typing my name.

Mango Publishing, established in 2014, publishes an eclectic list of books by diverse authors—both new and established voices—on topics ranging from business, personal growth, women's empowerment, LGBTQ+ studies, health, and spirituality to history, popular culture, time management, decluttering, lifestyle, mental wellness, aging, and sustainable living. We were named 2019 *and* 2020's #1 fastest growing independent publisher by *Publishers Weekly.* Our success is driven by our main goal, which is to publish high-quality books that will entertain readers as well as make a positive difference in their lives.

Our readers are our most important resource; we value your input, suggestions, and ideas. We'd love to hear from you—after all, we are publishing books for you!

Please stay in touch with us and follow us at:

Facebook: Mango Publishing

Twitter: @MangoPublishing

Instagram: @MangoPublishing

LinkedIn: Mango Publishing

Pinterest: Mango Publishing

Newsletter: mangopublishinggroup.com/newsletter

Join us on Mango's journey to reinvent publishing, one book at a time.

www.ingramcontent.com/pod-product-compliance
Lightning Source LLC
Jackson TN
JSHW030717280725
88197JS00001B/1

* 9 7 8 1 6 8 4 8 1 8 5 6 3 *